Pillsbury Best Chicken

COOKBOOK

Pillsbury Best Chicken
COOKBOOK

Favorite Recipes from
America's Most-Trusted Kitchens

Clarkson Potter/Publishers
New York

Credits

PILLSBURY PUBLICATIONS
The Pillsbury Company

Publisher: Sally Peters
Publication Manager: Diane B. Anderson
Senior Editor: Betsy Wray
Senior Food Editor: Andi Bidwell
Recipe Editor: Grace Wells
Contributing Writer: Mary Caldwell
Photography: Graham Brown Photography, Tad
    Ware Photography, Glenn Peterson Photography
Food Stylists: Sue Brosious, Sue Brue, JoAnn Cherry,
    Sharon Harding, Cindy Ojczyk, Amy Printy,
    Barb Standal
Recipe Typists: Julie Atkins, Bev Gustafson

PILLSBURY PUBLICATIONS

Publisher: Sally Peters
Publication Managers: Diane B. Anderson,
    William Monn

Senior Editors: Jackie Sheehan, Betsy Wray
Senior Food Editor: Andi Bidwell
Test Kitchen Coordinator: Pat Peterson
Circulation Manager: Karen Goodsell
Circulation Coordinator: Rebecca Bogema
Recipe Typists: Bev Gustafson, Mary Prokott,
    Nolan Vaughan

Bake-Off is a registered trademark of
    The Pillsbury Company.

CLARKSON POTTER/PUBLISHERS
The Crown Publishing Group

President and Publisher: Chip Gibson
Vice President-Editorial Director: Lauren Shakely
Senior Editor: Katie Workman
Editorial Assistant: Erica Youngren
Designer: Susan DeStaebler
Managing Editor: Laurie Stark
Associate Managing Editor: Amy Boorstein
Production Manager: Jane Searle
Publicist: Wendy Schuman

Published by Clarkson Potter/Publishers,
201 East 50th Street, New York, New York 10022.
Member of the Crown Publishing Group.

Random House, Inc. New York, Toronto,
London, Sydney, Auckland

www.randomhouse.com

CLARKSON N. POTTER, POTTER, and colophon are
registered trademarks of Random House, Inc.

Printed in the United States of America

Design by Susan DeStaebler

Library of Congress Cataloging-in-Publication Data
is available upon request

ISBN 0-517-70880-9

10 9 8 7 6 5 4 3

FRONTISPIECE: *Teriyaki Grilled
Chicken Kabobs page 215*

OPPOSITE: *Mandarin Chicken
Pockets page 67*

Contents

Chicken and Pepper Sandwiches page 76

Chicken and Cabbage Panade page 102

Light Sour Cream Chicken Enchiladas page 210

Caramelized Garlic Chicken page 182

Chicken Know-How

Home cooks and five-star chefs alike prize chicken for its mild flavor and amazing versatility. It works equally well for entrees and appetizers, for light summer lunches and hearty winter suppers, for casual picnic fare and dinner-party elegance. And it takes to the exotic seasonings of far-flung corners of the earth as easily as to the familiar flavors of simple home cooking.

What else does chicken have going for it? It's consistently one of the most affordable meats on the market. And it fits perfectly into today's nutritional guidelines. As people have become more careful about fat in the diet, chicken's popularity has grown. While beef consumption has declined in the last three decades, chicken consumption has seen a steady increase. More than 40% of American households serve chicken two or three times a week.

If you find yourself serving chicken that frequently, you'll appreciate the variety of recipes compiled here. Get down to basics with a simple, traditional Roast Chicken (page 205), or update your recipe file with Grilled Barbecue Chicken Pizza (page 223), in which two old favorites (barbecued chicken and pizza) team up to create an exciting new dinner. Go formal with a banquet-style Chicken Kiev (page 146) or cool off with a refreshing Summer Fruit and Chicken Salad (page 60). Whether you prefer to cook the bird whole or choose to follow the current U.S. trend of purchasing cut-up chicken parts, you'll find plenty to enjoy in this book.

Roast Chicken page 205

What the Label Means

In the supermarket, you're likely to find chicken labeled in the following ways.

Cornish game hens

The smallest and youngest of poultry commercially available in the United States, Cornish hens are 4 to 6 weeks old and weigh from ¾ pound to 2 pounds. Depending on the size, a single bird provides one or two servings.

Broiler/fryers

Broiler/fryers weigh in at 1½ to 3½ pounds and are 7 to 9 weeks old. They tend to be more tender than roasters.

Roasters

Varying from 4 to 8 pounds, roasters are about 16 weeks old. They have greater meat-to-bone ratio than the smaller birds and are ideal for roasting or cutting up and frying or baking.

Stewing hens

These tougher and older birds range from 4½ to 7 pounds and are usually 1 to 1½ years old. The meat is flavorful but stringy, so a stewer is best cooked slowly with moist heat, using methods such as braising, stewing or simmering for soup.

Oven-Fried Chicken page 204

Free-range chickens

The term "free-range" refers to chickens that have been allowed to roam rather than being confined to a coop. Some people say the exercise gives the meat better texture. These chickens are more expensive and are most often found on restaurant menus or in gourmet shops, though they sometimes can be found in the supermarket or at farmer's markets.

Kosher chicken

Kosher chicken, available in supermarkets as well as in kosher meat shops, has been butchered and processed according to Jewish law in the presence of a rabbi.

Butterflying a Chicken Breast

Butterflying is a simple cutting technique that yields a threefold benefit: It looks attractive, it cooks more quickly because the meat is thinner and it gives the illusion of a larger portion.

1. To butterfly a boneless chicken breast half, place the meat flat on a cutting board. Using a sharp knife, cut the chicken parallel to the work surface, through the center of the meat, but don't quite sever the two sections.

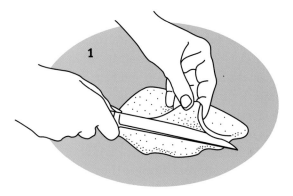

2. Open up the meat to form a "butterfly" shape.

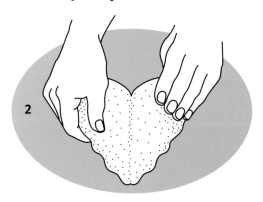

Boning a Chicken Breast

You can enjoy boneless chicken breasts at a more affordable price if you purchase bone-in breasts and do the work yourself. To bone a whole breast:

1. Remove the skin, if desired, and lay the breast, bone side up, on the work surface. Using a sharp knife, run the blade down the center to cut the thin membrane, exposing the keel bone (dark, spoon-shaped bone) and white cartilage.

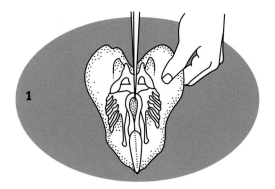

2. Remove the keel bone by placing your thumbs at the base and top of the keel bone. Bend the bone back until it breaks through the membrane. Run your finger under the edge of the keel bone and pull partially away from the breast. Pull down to remove the white cartilage.

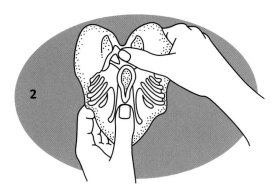

side of the breast. Locate the wishbone at the top of the center of the breast. Run the point of the knife close to the bone to remove the bone.

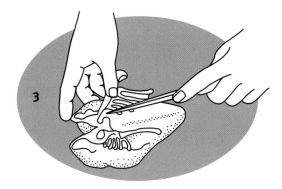

3. To remove the ribs, insert the point of a sharp knife under the ribs on one side of the breast and gradually scrape the meat away from the bones. Cut the ribs away. Cut through and under the shoulder joint and remove. Repeat with the other

4. Lay the breast flat and cut it in half along the cleft that contained the keel bone. Remove the white tendon and trim away the fat.

How Much Should I Buy?

Plan on ½ pound of bone-in chicken or ¼ pound of boneless meat per serving. One Cornish game hen will serve one or two people, depending on its size. If in doubt, buy a little extra—it usually doesn't hurt to have leftovers.

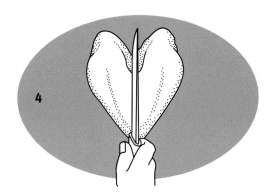

5. If desired, cut out the "tenderloin" section, a smaller, separate muscle that's easily removed from the main portion of the breast and can be cooked as separate little morsels or incorporated into the main dish.

Cutting Up a Whole Chicken

Not too many years ago, you paid a premium for pre-cut, packaged chicken parts. It was always most economical to buy a whole chicken and cut it up yourself. That's not so today; watch the specials to see which part is the best buy of the week.

Still, there are times when a whole chicken is least expensive or most convenient to purchase. If you want to cut it up yourself, here's how. (This method leaves the back as a separate piece that can be cooked along with the recipe or reserved for soup stock.)

1. Remove the neck and the giblets, if included, from the body cavity. Rinse the chicken and pat it dry.

2. Locate the ball and socket joint at the bird's shoulder. Using a sharp chef's knife, cut through the joint to remove the wings. If the knife meets resistance, you're trying to cut through bone; reposition the knife to find the joint, which can be cut easily.

3. If desired, further separate the wing into two or three sections, again cutting through the joint. Some cooks chop off the bony wing tips to save for soup stock; others leave them attached.

4. Slice the skin that connects the thigh to the body. Locate the ball and socket joint that connects the thigh to the body. Bend back the thigh from the body to pop the thigh out of the joint. Slice through the joint to remove the leg and thigh section. Again, if the knife meets resistance, move the knife so you're cutting directly through the joint, not bone.

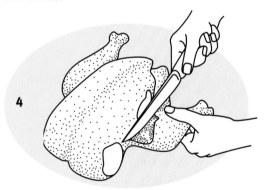

5. Separate the drumstick and thigh sections, if desired, by cutting through the connecting joint.

6. Cut hard through the ribs at both sides of the body to separate the front and the back. Set aside the back,

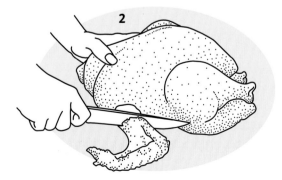

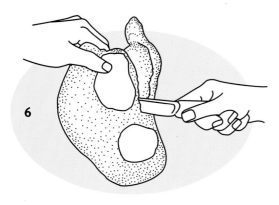

6

which doesn't have much meat, to use for soup stock.

7. Leave the breast whole, if desired. Or lay the breast flat on the work surface, skin side up, and cut hard through the center, cutting through the bone, to separate the breast into left and right halves. (This will be easier if you first remove the keel bone, as described in Boning a Chicken Breast on page 10.) You can slice each breast portion in half crosswise to make more small portions of white meat.

Carving a Whole Chicken

Let the cooked chicken rest, out of the oven, for 10 to 15 minutes before carving. This lets the juices redistribute throughout the bird and eases carving.

1. Cut through the joint between the thigh and the body of the bird to

remove the leg. Separate the drumstick from the thigh. For a small bird, serve the pieces whole. For a large roaster, you may want to further cut the dark meat into slices.

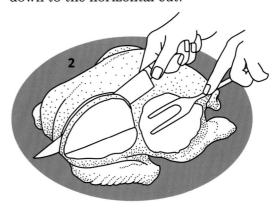

1

2. Make a deep horizontal cut into the breast meat, slicing close to the bone to loosen the meat underneath, just above the wing. Beginning near the front of the breast, cut thin slices down to the horizontal cut.

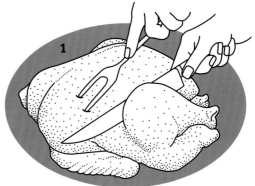

2

3. Cut the wings through the joint.

Cooking Methods

Baking

Preheat the oven. Rinse chicken parts and pat them dry, then follow the recipe for seasoning, and so on. Chicken parts take about an hour at 350°F., slightly less at 375°F.

Braising

Brown the chicken in a pan on the stovetop, then cook, tightly covered, over low heat in a small amount of liquid until the meat is fork-tender, 45 minutes to 1 hour for chicken parts with bones in.

Broiling

Preheat the broiler. Rinse the chicken parts and pat them dry. Season according to the recipe. Place the chicken, skin side down, on the preheated broiler and broil until browned, about 30 minutes. Turn the chicken over and continue to broil until the skin is nicely browned and the meat is cooked through, 15 to 25 minutes.

Poaching

Simmer the chicken in a flavorful liquid, about 15 minutes per pound. You can use chicken broth, wine or water flavored with seasonings or aromatic vegetables such as onions and garlic. This is a great no-fat-added way to cook chicken, especially breasts.

Grilling

Grilling chicken is simple in theory but involves art as well as science. Because the thickness of the meat, style of the grill and intensity of the heat will affect the grilling time, watch the chicken carefully so it cooks through but doesn't dry out or burn. Some general grilling guidelines:

- Whole chicken (about 3½ pounds)—cooking can be speeded

Chicken Parts	Cup Amount
3- to 4-pound fryer	3 to 4 cups cooked, cubed chicken
2 whole chicken breasts (1½ pounds with skin and bone)	2 cups cooked, cubed chicken
¾ pound chicken breast (boned, skinned)	2 cups cooked, cubed chicken
5-ounce can chunk chicken (drained, flaked)	1 cup

slightly by splitting the chicken entirely in half or splitting it along the backbone and flattening it open. Grill about 1 hour over indirect heat, or until juices run clear when the skin between the thigh and the body is pierced. There's no need to turn the meat over when using the indirect grilling method.

- Broiler-fryer chicken halves (1¼ to 1½ pounds each)—grill over direct heat for 40 to 50 minutes, or until no pink remains and juices run clear when you cut into the thickest part of the meat. Turn the pieces over halfway through the cooking time.

- Chicken breast halves, thighs and drumsticks with bone in (2 to 2½ pounds total)—grill over direct heat for 35 to 45 minutes, or until no pink remains and juices run clear when you cut into the thickest part of the meat. (Smaller pieces may cook more quickly.) Turn the pieces over halfway through the cooking time.

- Boneless chicken breast halves and thighs (about ¼ pound each)—grill over direct heat for 10 to 18 minutes, or until no pink remains and juices run clear when you cut into the breast. Boneless thighs may cook slightly more quickly. Turn the pieces over halfway through the cooking time.

- Chicken wings—grill over direct heat for 25 to 35 minutes, or until no pink remains and the juices run clear. Turn the pieces over halfway through the cooking time.

Microwaving

In general, microwave cooking is better for small to medium amounts of chicken; roasting a whole bird is better done conventionally. Cooking times vary according to the power of your microwave, the amount of meat, how it's cut up and what other ingredients cook along with it.

Grilled Raspberry Chicken Spinach Salad page 29

For example, to obtain 2 to 2½ cups of cooked, cubed chicken, place 2 whole chicken breasts (1½ to 2 pounds) in a 12 × 8-inch (2-quart) dish; cover the chicken with microwave-safe waxed paper. Microwave it on high for 8 to 10 minutes or until it is no longer pink and the juices run clear. Halfway through cooking, rotate the dish one-half turn and rearrange the chicken. Cool the chicken and cut it into cubes or bite-sized pieces.

Sautéing

Sautéing can be used for any chicken part, but is best for cut-up or boneless meat. The meat is browned in fat on the stovetop, developing a golden exterior. Heat the pan and the oil, then add the meat, being sure not to crowd the pan. Cook the first side until it's browned and the edges start to look white. Flip the meat and continue to cook until the second side is browned and the chicken is white and opaque throughout.

Stir-Frying

Cut boneless, skinless chicken into small pieces of uniform size. Heat a wok (or large skillet) for several minutes over high heat, then add a "girdle" of oil inside the wok near the top: Trickle the oil in a circle around the top inside edge and let the oil drip down to coat the wok. (Peanut oil or corn oil works best; olive oil has a low smoking point and tends to burn too quickly for high-heat wok cookery.) Add the chopped meat, a little at a time, to the center of the wok. As it begins to cook, push it up the sides of the pan and add more chicken to the center. Stir and fry until the meat is browned outside and no longer pink in the center.

Light Lemon Chicken page 135

Storage and Safety

Purchasing and Storing Chicken

At the supermarket, check the "sell-by" date on the package. Once you have the chicken home, plan to use it or freeze it within two days (one is better), regardless of the freshness date on the package.

Freezing Raw Chicken

Before freezing raw chicken, remove the grocery store wrap (or wrap over it with a heavier material) if you plan to store the chicken for more than a couple of weeks. Rewrap the pieces individually in heavy-duty plastic wrap, heavy-duty aluminum foil or freezer paper. For extra protection, and to prevent individual pieces from becoming "lost" and wasted in the freezer, package the individually wrapped pieces together in a heavy-duty, self-sealing freezer bag labeled with the date and the contents. Foods frozen at 0°F. will remain safe indefinitely, but the texture, flavor and color will deteriorate over time. For best results, use whole frozen chickens within one year, parts within nine months and giblets or ground meat within four months.

If the packaging is not tight or the wrapper becomes torn, "freezer burn" (dehydrated, discolored patches) may result. Although freezer burn looks and tastes unpleasant, it is not dangerous. Use a sharp knife to cut away the affected areas.

Storing Leftovers

Put food away as soon as possible after the meal, but definitely within two hours. Cooked leftover chicken can be refrigerated for three to four days.

Package cooked leftover chicken in shallow containers and seal tightly. Frozen leftovers will be best if used within three to six months. Longer freezing will not affect safety, but the flavor, texture and color may deteriorate.

Is It Done?

To test doneness in a whole roasted chicken, pierce the skin that connects the thigh to the body and watch the juices that emerge. If the juices run clear, the bird is done. If there's still any tinge of pinkness in the liquid, return the bird to the oven.

Whole roasted chickens should reach an internal temperature (measured with a meat thermometer) of 180°F.; stuffing should reach 165°F. Parts should reach 160°F.

Thawing Chicken

The best way to thaw frozen chicken is to do it slowly, in the refrigerator, on a plate to catch any drips. Count on about 12 hours to defrost 2 to 3 pounds of chicken.

Or set the frozen chicken, still in its wrapper, in a bowl of cold water on the counter. If the wrapper is torn, put the whole package into a plastic bag and seal it tightly before submerging it. Change the water frequently or add ice cubes to keep it cold; bacteria that cause food-borne illness multiply rapidly at temperatures above 40°F. Do **not** thaw chicken at room temperature, and do not thaw it in hot water.

Frozen chicken can also be defrosted in the microwave oven; follow the manufacturer's instructions for length of time. Since the outer edges of the food may actually begin to cook while the center is still defrosting, cook microwave-thawed foods immediately.

Safe Handling Tips

- Bring chicken directly home from the market and store it in the coldest part of the refrigerator. Set the package on a plate or dish to catch any drips, which could contaminate other foods.
- Handling raw poultry increases the chances of contamination, so handle it as little as possible. Refrigerate chicken in its original wrapper. If the wrapper becomes torn, overwrap the package with a tightly sealed plastic bag.
- Wash your hands thoroughly before and after handling raw chicken.
- Use hot, soapy water to wash knives, cutting boards and anything else that has come into contact with raw chicken.
- Liquids that have been used to marinate raw chicken or to brush onto chicken as it cooks must be discarded; if the liquid is to be used as a sauce at the table, boil the mixture to eliminate risk of contamination.
- Stuff the bird just before cooking—not the night before.
- Keep raw chicken cold or cook it completely. Do not partially cook chicken, then hold it to finish cooking later.
- Cook chicken until the juices run clear and no trace of pink remains (see page 17 for internal temperatures).
- Remove any stuffing from the cavity before serving.
- Refrigerate leftovers promptly and store chicken and stuffing separately.

Roasted Chicken and Vegetables Provençal page 181

To Skin or Not to Skin

A considerable portion of chicken's fat is found in the skin. The good news is that it doesn't matter from a fat-consumption standpoint whether or not you cook the chicken with the skin on, as long as you don't eat the skin.

Cooking the chicken with the skin on can help to protect the meat inside and keep it more moist; on the other hand, if seasonings are applied to the skin, some of the flavor will be lost if the skin is removed after cooking. A compromise suggested in some recipes is to loosen the skin, rub flavorings underneath, cook the poultry, then remove the skin after cooking.

How to Remove Skin

- To remove skin from the breast or thigh, loosen the skin by running your fingers or a small knife under the skin, being careful not to pierce the flesh. Gently pull the skin off.

- To skin a drumstick, grasp the small end in one hand and pull the skin down, away from the meaty portion and "inside out" over the little end. It may help to use a heavy paper towel or clean dish towel if the skin is slippery.

- You could follow the thigh technique for the "drummette" end of the wing, though it's hardly worth the bother. Likewise, just leave the skin on the smaller portion of the wing.

Using the Nutrition Information in This Book

At the end of each recipe, you'll find detailed nutrition information, based on current information from the U.S. Department of Agriculture and food manufacturers' labels. We include calories per serving as well as the amount of fat, cholesterol, sodium and dietary fiber.

You'll also find dietary exchanges— the nutritional accounting system commonly used by people with diabetes. This information is based on the **1995 Exchange Lists for Meal Planning** by the American Diabetes Association and the American Dietetic Association. If you have questions about the dietary exchange system, call the American Dietetic Association at 1-800-366-1655.

How We Calculate Nutrition Information

When we calculate nutrition we:

- Use the **first** ingredient mentioned when the recipe gives options. For example, if "butter or margarine" is listed, butter would be calculated.
- Use the **larger** amount of an ingredient when there's a range.
- Add in garnishing or "if desired" ingredients if they are included in the ingredient list.
- Include the estimated amount of marinade absorbed during preparation.

Chicken Nutrition

	Weight (Uncooked, with bone)	Calories*	Fat (g)	Cholesterol (mg)	Protein (g)
Breast half	6 oz.	140	3	75	27
Breast half with skin	6 oz.	190	8	80	29
Drumstick	4 oz.	70	2	40	12
Drumstick with skin	4 oz.	110	6	45	14
Thigh	4 oz.	110	6	50	13
Thigh with skin	4 oz.	150	10	60	16
Wing	3 oz.	40	2	20	6
Wing with skin	3 oz.	100	7	30	9

*Nutrition figures are for cooked, edible portions.

Tip Talk

Throughout this book you will find helpful hints accompanying each recipe. The information falls into the following categories:

Recipe Fact

imparts a bit of culinary background.

About (Ingredient)

shares a nugget of information about a component of the recipe.

Kitchen Tip

explains the most expeditious way to prepare certain ingredients or carry out special techniques.

Healthy Hint

recommends easy ways to reduce fat or calories in the recipe.

Ingredient Substitution

proposes satisfactory alternatives in case your pantry lacks a specific item called for in the recipe.

Make-Ahead Tip

tells how much of the preparation can be completed in advance.

Recipe Variation

outlines an easy way to transform the recipe at hand into a new and different dish.

Make It Special

offers easy ideas for garnishes and embellishments for the entree.

Menu Suggestion

lists ideas for dishes to complement the particular chicken recipe.

In addition, three special "flags" help categorize recipes at a glance:

30 Minutes or Less indicates recipes that require less than half an hour to get to the table.

Low-Fat denotes recipes that have 10 grams of fat or less per serving.

Editor's Choice gives you insider information about our staff's very favorite dishes.

Menu Magic

With more than 175 chicken recipes to choose from, **Pillsbury's Best Chicken Cookbook** offers a wealth of take-off points for fabulous meals. To get you started, we've created 20 theme-based menus. Each includes a recipe from this book plus ideas for purchased accompaniments or quickly assembled side dishes to round out the meal.

Main-Dish Salads

Party on the Porch

Chicken and Vegetables with Dijon
   Vinaigrette (p. 30)
Bran muffins
Selection of sliced cheeses
Fresh berries with whipped
   topping
Iced tea

Brown Derby Salad Luncheon

Cobb Salad (p. 43)
Hard rolls or sourdough bread
Watermelon wedges
Brownies a la mode
Sparkling mineral water

Casual Family Fiesta

Grilled Chicken Taco Salad (p. 52)
Corn muffins
Pickled hot cherry peppers
Frozen fruit bars
Tropical punch or flavored iced
   tea

Book Club Luncheon

Chicken and Wild Rice Salad
   (p. 32)
Whole wheat dinner rolls or
   croissants
Sliced cantaloupe and honeydew
   melon
Cheesecake
Wine, sparkling water

Grilled Chicken Taco Salad page 52

Bacon Cheddar Chicken Fillet Melt page 68

Sandwiches

Satisfying Sandwich Supper

Bacon Cheddar Chicken Fillet
    Melt (p. 68)
Creamy coleslaw salad
Chips
Frozen yogurt with cookies
Milk, lemonade

South-of-the-Border Sandwich Supper

Chicken Quesadillas (p. 83)
Spanish rice
Refried beans
Avocado slices for garnish
Fresh sliced strawberries
    drizzled with honey
Ice water with lemon or lime slices

After-Shopping Supper

Hot Chicken Hoagie (p. 86)
Potato salad
Bread and butter pickles
    and carrot sticks
Carrot cake
Fruit punch, soft drinks

Soups, Stews and Chilies

Hearty Chili Supper

Chunky Chicken Chili (p. 114)
Warm cheese-filled flour tortillas
Red and green grapes
Milk

Down-Home Southern Supper

Oven Chicken Stew (p. 122)
Cranberry relish
Baking powder biscuits
Pecan pie
Iced tea

Invite the Neighbors for Soup

Spicy Chicken Bean Soup (p. 126)
Tortilla chips with guacamole dip
Cocktail bread slices with sliced
    Monterey jack cheese
Fresh strawberry shortcake with
    whipped topping
Beer, wine, soft drinks

Chunky Chicken Chili page 114

Tangy Sesame Chicken page 174

Skillet and Stir-Fry

Anytime Family Supper

Easy Chicken Tetrazzini (p. 158)
Italian breadsticks
Spinach salad with Italian dressing
Chocolate cake
Milk

Stir-Fry Dinner

Easy Moo Goo Gai Pan (p. 157)
Egg rolls with sweet-and-sour or
    mustard sauce
Orange or lime sherbet with
    fortune cookies
Hot tea

Chinese "Take-Out" at Home

Tangy Sesame Chicken (p. 174)
Shredded vegetable salad with
    sweet-and-sour dressing
Egg drop soup
Custard pudding with almond flavor
Wine, soft drinks

Baked and Roasted

Special Occasion Luncheon

Crescent Chicken Newburg
    (p. 194)
Sliced fresh tomatoes with basil
    garnish
Lemon meringue pie
Wine coolers and iced tea with
    lemon

Company Casserole Supper

Chicken, Artichoke and Rice
    Casserole (p. 188)
Steamed broccoli
Soft breadsticks
Sliced fresh fruit
Chocolate pudding with whipped
    topping
Wine, soft drinks

Crescent Chicken Newburg page 194

Grilled and Broiled

Taste of Indonesia

Indonesian Chicken (p. 226)
White or brown rice
Sliced tomatoes and cucumbers
    with yogurt
Coconut macaroons
Pineapple juice

Italian Supper on the Patio

Italian Chicken and Vegetable Grill
    (p. 234)
Fresh fruit salad
Focaccia or Italian rolls
Spumoni ice cream with chocolate
    biscotti cookies
Cappuccino

Summertime Garden Supper

Grilled Rosemary Chicken
    (p. 225)
New potatoes with chives
Steamed fresh green beans
Fresh raspberries and cream
Iced tea with mint

Come for Kabobs

Teriyaki Grilled Chicken Kabobs
    (p. 215)
White rice or fried rice
Steamed fresh asparagus with
    sesame seed garnish
Grilled pineapple slices
Hot tea with lemon

Italian Chicken and Vegetable Grill page 234

Glazes and Rubs

Summer Chicken Grill Get-Together

Chicken grilled with choice of
    glaze or rub (pp. 245-249)
Garlic French bread
Corn on the cob
Potato salad or creamed new
    potatoes
Watermelon wedges
Strawberry shortcake
Iced tea and lemonade

in-Dish Salads

Broaden your chicken salad horizons. In addition to traditional-style salads dressed with mayonnaise, this chapter presents poultry in guises that run the gamut from mild, fruit-accented lunches to peppery, substantial dinner fare. And while chicken salad offers the quintessential solution for cool summer meals, the possibilities here include warm combinations just right for year-round dining.

Main-Dish Salads

Previous page: Grilled Raspberry Chicken Spinach Salad page 29

Grilled Raspberry Chicken Spinach Salad

Prep Time: 25 minutes

• 30 min. or less   • low-fat   • editor's choice

Glaze and Dressing
1 cup red raspberry preserves
⅓ cup red wine vinegar

Salad
4 boneless, skinless chicken
  breast halves

8 cups torn spinach
2 cups melon balls or cubes
1 cup fresh raspberries or
  halved small strawberries
1 small red onion, thinly sliced

1. Heat grill. In small bowl, combine preserves and vinegar; blend well. Reserve ⅓ cup for glaze. Set remaining mixture aside for dressing.

2. When ready to grill, oil grill rack. Place chicken on gas grill over medium heat or on charcoal grill 4 to 6 inches from medium coals. Brush chicken with reserved glaze; cook 5 minutes. Turn chicken over; brush with glaze. Cook an additional 3 to 7 minutes, or until chicken is fork-tender and juices run clear, brushing occasionally with glaze.

3. Meanwhile, arrange spinach, melon, raspberries and onion on 4 individual plates. Slice each chicken breast crosswise; arrange over spinach mixture. Drizzle with dressing.

Yield: 4 servings

Tip: To broil, place chicken on broiler pan and broil 4 to 6 inches from heat using times provided above as a guide.

Nutrition Information Per Serving

Serving Size: ¼ of Recipe • Calories 420 • Calories from Fat 35 • Total Fat 4 g
Saturated Fat 1 g • Cholesterol 75 mg • Sodium 190 mg • Dietary Fiber 7 g
Dietary Exchanges: 4 Fruit, 2 Vegetable, 4 Very Lean Meat OR
4 Carbohydrate, 2 Vegetable, 4 Very Lean Meat

Kitchen Tip

To make the preserves easier to brush on the chicken, microwave them on HIGH for about 15 seconds.

Make It Special

Garnish each serving with a fresh mint sprig and an orange slice slit to the center and given a twist.

Menu Suggestion

Serve with a crisp white wine and slices of a crusty baguette.

Chicken and Vegetables with Dijon Vinaigrette

Prep Time: 30 minutes

Salad
4 boneless, skinless chicken breast halves
½ teaspoon peppered seasoned salt or seasoned salt
4 medium new red potatoes, quartered
¼ teaspoon salt
½ lb. whole green beans
1 medium red bell pepper, cut into thin strips

1 medium yellow summer squash, cut into 2-inch thin strips

Dressing
⅓ cup chopped walnuts, toasted*
¼ cup olive oil or vegetable oil
⅓ cup white wine vinegar
2 tablespoons Dijon mustard
2 teaspoons sugar

Grill Directions: 1. Heat grill. Sprinkle chicken with peppered seasoned salt. When ready to grill, place chicken on gas grill over medium heat or on charcoal grill 4 to 6 inches from medium-high coals. Cook 10 to 15 minutes, or until chicken is fork-tender and juices run clear, turning once.

2. Meanwhile, place potatoes in large skillet; add ½ inch of water and the salt. Bring to a boil. Reduce heat to medium; cover and cook 5 minutes. Add green beans; cover and cook an additional 6 to 8 minutes, or until vegetables are crisp-tender. Add bell pepper and squash; cook 2 to 4 minutes, or until all vegetables are just tender. Drain.

3. In small jar with tight-fitting lid, combine all dressing ingredients; shake well. Cut warm chicken crosswise into slices. Arrange chicken and vegetables on large platter; drizzle with dressing.

Yield: 4 servings

Broiler Directions: 1. Sprinkle chicken with peppered seasoned salt. Place on broiler pan.
2. Broil 4 to 6 inches from heat for 10 to 15 minutes, or until chicken is fork-tender and juices run clear, turning once. Continue as directed above.

*Tip: To toast walnuts, spread on cookie sheet; bake at 350°F. for 5 to 7 minutes, or until golden brown, stirring occasionally. Or, spread walnuts in thin layer in microwave-safe pie pan. Microwave on HIGH for 4 to 7 minutes, or until golden brown, stirring frequently.

Nutrition Information Per Serving

Serving Size: ¼ of Recipe • Calories 460 Calories from Fat 220 • Total Fat 24 g
Saturated Fat 3 g • Cholesterol 75 mg • Sodium 450 mg • Dietary Fiber 6 g
Dietary Exchanges: 1 Starch, 2 Vegetable, 4 Lean Meat, 2½ Fat OR
1 Carbohydrate, 2 Vegetable, 4 Lean Meat, 2½ Fat

Make-Ahead Tip

Several hours ahead, combine all the dressing ingredients except the walnuts in a jar with a tight-fitting lid. Just before serving, add the walnuts and shake well, then drizzle the dressing over the chicken and vegetables.

Chicken and Vegetables with Dijon Vinaigrette

Chicken and Wild Rice Salad

Prep Time: 15 minutes
(Ready in 3 hours 30 minutes)

1 cup uncooked wild rice
½ cup salad dressing or
    mayonnaise
⅓ cup sour cream
½ teaspoon salt
¼ teaspoon dried marjoram
    leaves, crushed
⅛ teaspoon white pepper
2 cups cubed cooked chicken
½ cup diagonally sliced celery

½ cup chopped red bell
    pepper
½ cup sliced fresh mushrooms
¼ cup diagonally sliced green
    onions
6 leaves lettuce
1 large tomato, cut into wedges
¼ cup slivered almonds,
    toasted*

About White Pepper

White pepper is just black pepper that has been allowed to ripen slightly longer and then has been hulled. Its flavor is milder than that of the black variety.

Healthy Hint

To lower fat by 3 grams per serving in this recipe, substitute nonfat sour cream or nonfat plain yogurt for the sour cream.

1. Cook wild rice according to package directions. Drain; refrigerate 30 minutes, or until chilled.

2. Meanwhile, in small bowl, combine salad dressing, sour cream, salt, marjoram and pepper; blend well.

3. In large bowl, combine cooked rice, chicken, celery, bell pepper, mushrooms and green onions. Add mayonnaise mixture; toss gently. Cover; refrigerate 2 to 3 hours to blend flavors.

4. Arrange lettuce on 4 individual plates. Spoon salad over lettuce. Garnish with tomato wedges and toasted almonds.

Yield: 6 servings

*Tip: To toast almonds, spread on cookie sheet; bake at 350°F. for 5 to 7 minutes, or until golden brown, stirring occasionally. Or, spread almonds in thin layer in microwave-safe pie pan. Microwave on HIGH for 4 to 7 minutes, or until golden brown, stirring frequently.

Nutrition Information Per Serving

Serving Size: ⅙ of Recipe • Calories 330 • Calories from Fat 140 • Total Fat 16 g
Saturated Fat 4 g • Cholesterol 55 mg • Sodium 380 mg • Dietary Fiber 3 g
Dietary Exchanges: 2 Starch, 2 Very Lean Meat, 2 Fat OR
2 Carbohydrate, 2 Very Lean Meat, 2 Fat

Chicken and Wild Rice Salad

Chicken Gazpacho Salad

Prep Time: 30 minutes

3 tablespoons lemon juice
3 tablespoons olive oil or vegetable oil
1½ teaspoons chopped fresh basil or ½ teaspoon dried basil leaves
¼ teaspoon salt
3 to 4 drops hot pepper sauce
1 garlic clove, minced, or ½ teaspoon chopped garlic in water

3 green onions, sliced
2 medium tomatoes, seeded, chopped
1 small cucumber, halved lengthwise, thinly sliced
1 medium green bell pepper, chopped
4 boneless, skinless chicken breast halves
4 cups torn salad greens

Grill Directions: 1. Heat grill. In medium bowl, combine all ingredients except chicken and salad greens; mix well.
2. Place 1 chicken breast half between 2 pieces of plastic wrap or waxed paper. Working from center, gently pound chicken with flat side of meat mallet or rolling pin until about ¼ inch thick; remove wrap. Repeat with remaining chicken breast halves.
3. When ready to grill, place chicken breast halves on gas grill over medium heat or on charcoal grill 4 to 6 inches from medium coals. Cook 8 to 10 minutes, or until chicken is fork-tender and juices run clear, turning once. Cut chicken crosswise into ½-inch slices.
4. Arrange greens on 4 individual plates. Stir vegetable mixture. Using slotted spoon, arrange vegetable mixture over greens. Arrange chicken slices over vegetable mixture; spoon liquid from vegetable mixture over chicken.

Yield: 4 servings

Broiler Directions: 1. Prepare recipe as directed above. Place chicken breast halves on broiler pan.

2. Broil 4 to 6 inches from heat for 8 to 10 minutes, or until chicken is fork-tender and juices run clear, turning once. Continue as directed above.

Nutrition Information Per Serving

Serving Size: ¼ of Recipe • Calories 280 • Calories from Fat 130 • Total Fat 14 g
Saturated Fat 2 g • Cholesterol 75 mg • Sodium 220 mg • Dietary Fiber 3 g
Dietary Exchanges: 2 Vegetable, 2 Lean Meat, 1 Fat

Make-Ahead Tip

Grill the chicken and prepare the vegetable mixture up to a day in advance and refrigerate them separately; assemble just before serving.

Chicken Salad for a Crowd

Prep Time: 30 minutes
(Ready in 4 hours 30 minutes)

12 oz. (2 cups) uncooked orzo or rosamarina (rice-shaped pasta)
2 cups mayonnaise or salad dressing
¼ cup half-and-half
1 tablespoon salt
2 teaspoons white pepper

2 tablespoons lemon juice
4 cups cubed cooked chicken
2 cups seedless green grapes, halved
2 cups (1 large) chopped seeded cucumber
1 cup chopped celery

1. Cook orzo to desired doneness as directed on package. Drain; rinse with cold water.

2. In large bowl, combine mayonnaise, half-and-half, salt, pepper and lemon juice. Stir in cooked orzo and all remaining ingredients; mix well. Cover; refrigerate at least 4 hours or overnight.

Yield: 25 (½-cup) servings

Nutrition Information Per Serving

Serving Size: ½ Cup • Calories 240 • Calories from Fat 140 • Total Fat 16 g
Saturated Fat 3 g • Cholesterol 30 mg • Sodium 380 mg • Dietary Fiber 1 g
Dietary Exchanges: 1 Starch, 1 Lean Meat, 2½ Fat OR
1 Carbohydrate, 1 Lean Meat, 2½ Fat

About Orzo

Orzo, a rice-shaped pasta, also goes by the name rosamarina, which means "rose of the sea."

Kitchen Tip

To seed a cucumber, cut it in half lengthwise and scrape out the seeds with a teaspoon, small melon baller or grapefruit spoon.

Healthy Hint

Substitute low-fat for regular mayonnaise and skim milk for half-and-half to slash the fat per serving from 16 grams to 3 grams.

Chicken, Corn and Black Bean Salad

About Chili Powder

Not all chili powders are the same; the ingredient listing on the package will tell you what you're getting. Cooking purists prefer pure ground chili peppers. Other chili powders are a blend of seasonings that may include ground chilies, cumin and possibly salt. The degree of heat also varies considerably. Experiment to find which type you prefer.

Kitchen Tip

To extract the most juice from a fresh lime, roll it on the counter or microwave it for about 10 seconds before cutting it.

Make-Ahead Tip

Store the prepared salad up to two days in the refrigerator.

Menu Suggestion

Serve this sweet-spicy salad with sliced fresh tomatoes and crusty sourdough rolls.

Prep Time: 20 minutes

Dressing
½ cup apricot preserves (chop large pieces)
¼ cup lime juice
1 tablespoon oil
1 teaspoon chili powder
⅛ to ¼ teaspoon ground red pepper (cayenne)

Salad
2 cups cubed cooked chicken
1 medium red or green bell pepper, chopped
2 cups frozen whole kernel corn, thawed
1 (15-oz.) can black beans, drained, rinsed
5 to 6 leaves Boston lettuce

1. In small bowl, combine all dressing ingredients; blend well.

2. In large bowl, combine all salad ingredients except lettuce. Add dressing; blend well. Arrange lettuce on 5 individual plates. Spoon salad over lettuce.

Yield: 5 servings

Nutrition Information Per Serving
Serving Size: ⅕ of Recipe • Calories 360 • Calories from Fat 70 • Total Fat 8 g
Saturated Fat 2 g • Cholesterol 50 mg • Sodium 75 mg • Dietary Fiber 7 g
Dietary Exchanges: 2 Starch, 1 Fruit, 1 Vegetable, 2 Lean Meat, ½ Fat OR
3 Carbohydrate, 1 Vegetable, 2 Lean Meat, ½ Fat

Chicken Tortellini Salad

Prep Time: 10 minutes
(Ready in 3 hours 10 minutes)

2 boneless, skinless chicken
   breast halves, cut crosswise
   into thin strips
2 tablespoons purchased
   Caesar salad dressing
1 (9-oz.) pkg. uncooked
   refrigerated cheese tortellini
½ cup drained oil-packed sun-
   dried tomatoes, chopped

2 tablespoons capers, if
   desired
1 (6-oz.) jar marinated
   artichoke hearts, drained,
   halved
⅓ cup purchased Caesar salad
   dressing
2 cups torn spinach

1. Place chicken and 2 tablespoons salad dressing in small glass dish or resealable plastic bag; turn chicken to coat all sides. Cover dish or seal bag; refrigerate at least 1 hour.
2. Meanwhile, cook tortellini to desired doneness as directed on package. Drain; rinse with cold water.
3. Place chicken and salad dressing mixture in medium skillet. Cook chicken over medium-high heat until no longer pink and lightly browned; drain.
4. In large bowl, combine chicken, tortellini, tomatoes, capers and artichoke hearts. Add ⅓ cup dressing; toss to coat. Refrigerate at least 2 hours to blend flavors. Just before serving, add spinach leaves; toss gently.

Yield: 6 (1¼-cup) servings

Nutrition Information Per Serving
Serving Size: 1¼ Cups • Calories 280 • Calories from Fat 110 • Total Fat 12 g
Saturated Fat 3 g • Cholesterol 50 mg • Sodium 430 mg • Dietary Fiber 4 g
Dietary Exchanges: 1½ Starch, 1 Vegetable, 1½ Lean Meat, 1½ Fat OR
1½ Carbohydrate, 1 Vegetable, 1½ Lean Meat, 1½ Fat

About Capers

Capers, the pickled flower bud of a bush that grows in the Mediterranean region, add a piquant note to this salad. For greatest impact, stir in the capers immediately before serving.

Kitchen Tip

Spinach grows in sandy soil and tends to be gritty unless you buy it pre-washed. Soak the leaves in a large bowl of cold water for at least 10 minutes, then lift them into a colander to drain, leaving the grit behind in the bowl. Rinse the bowl and repeat the soaking process until no trace of sand remains when you lift out the leaves.

low-fat

Chinese-Style Salad

Prep Time: 40 minutes

About Snow Peas

Snow peas, a favorite ingredient in Chinese cooking, are thin-skinned edible pods enclosing tiny peas. To prepare them, snap off the little stem and peel off the strings that run along each side of the pod.

About Rice Vinegar

Rice vinegar, widely used in Asian cooking, has a mild, slightly sweet flavor.

Recipe Variation

Vary the texture and flavor of this salad by experimenting with different vegetable combinations. Try Chinese cabbage, for example, instead of the romaine lettuce, and substitute bean sprouts for some of the carrots. Add crunch with a small can of sliced water chestnuts.

$\frac{1}{3}$ **cup purchased teriyaki sauce**
3 tablespoons rice vinegar
1 teaspoon sesame seed
$\frac{1}{4}$ **teaspoon coarsely ground black pepper**
4 boneless, skinless chicken breast halves
1 large head romaine lettuce, thinly sliced (about 8 cups)

2 medium carrots, cut into julienne strips (2 × $\frac{1}{4}$ × $\frac{1}{4}$ inches)
1 small red bell pepper, cut into julienne strips (2 × $\frac{1}{4}$ × $\frac{1}{4}$ inches)
4 oz. (1 cup) fresh snow pea pods, cut diagonally in half

Grill Directions: 1. Heat grill. In medium bowl, combine teriyaki sauce, vinegar, sesame seed and pepper; mix well. Reserve $\frac{1}{4}$ cup for dressing. Add chicken to remaining mixture; toss to coat. Let stand 5 to 10 minutes at room temperature to marinate.
2. When ready to grill, remove chicken from marinade; discard marinade. Place chicken on gas grill over medium heat or on charcoal grill 4 to 6 inches from medium coals. Cook 10 to 15 minutes, or until chicken is fork-tender and juices run clear, turning once.
3. Meanwhile, in large bowl, combine lettuce, carrots, bell pepper and pea pods. Add reserved $\frac{1}{4}$ cup dressing; toss to coat. Arrange on 4 individual plates.
4. Slice each chicken breast half crosswise into slices; do not separate slices. Fan chicken slices; arrange 1 breast half on lettuce mixture on each plate.

Yield: 4 servings

Broiler Directions: 1. Marinate chicken as directed above. Place chicken on broiler pan.

38 Pillsbury: Best Chicken Cookbook

Chinese-Style Salad

2. Broil 4 to 6 inches from heat for 10 to 15 minutes, or until chicken is fork-tender and juices run clear, turning once. Continue as directed above.

Nutrition Information Per Serving
Serving Size: ¼ of Recipe • Calories 210 • Calories from Fat 35 • Total Fat 4 g
Saturated Fat 1 g • Cholesterol 75 mg • Sodium 630 mg • Dietary Fiber 5 g
Dietary Exchanges: 2½ Vegetable, 4 Very Lean Meat

Light Caesar Chicken Salad

Prep Time: 25 minutes

Recipe Fact

The original Caesar salad, traditionally prepared tableside in restaurants, flavors romaine lettuce with anchovies and a dressing of raw egg and Worcestershire sauce. Our version reduces the fat in the dressing and eliminates the raw egg because of food safety concerns but adds chicken slices to make the salad a satisfying entree.

About Anchovy Paste

Anchovy paste, a spreadable mixture of anchovies and salt, saves you the trouble of mashing up the little fish fillets yourself. A little goes a long way, but even people who dislike anchovies may love dishes such as Caesar salad that rely on just a tiny bit of anchovy for depth of flavor.

Dressing

2 tablespoons grated Parmesan cheese
2 tablespoons olive oil
2 tablespoons lemon juice
2 tablespoons water
1 tablespoon reduced-fat sour cream
1 teaspoon Worcestershire sauce
1 teaspoon Dijon mustard
$\frac{1}{2}$ teaspoon anchovy paste or $\frac{1}{4}$ teaspoon salt
$\frac{1}{4}$ teaspoon pepper
2 garlic cloves, minced

Salad

4 boneless, skinless chicken breast halves
1 teaspoon salt-free garlic-herb blend
10 cups torn romaine lettuce
1 medium tomato, cut into 8 wedges

Grill Directions: 1. Heat grill. In medium bowl, combine all dressing ingredients; blend well.

2. Place 1 chicken breast half between 2 pieces of plastic wrap or waxed paper. Working from center, gently pound chicken with flat side of meat mallet or rolling pin until about $\frac{1}{4}$ inch thick; remove wrap. Repeat with remaining chicken breast halves.

3. When ready to grill, lightly sprinkle both sides of each chicken breast half with herb blend. Place chicken on gas grill over medium heat or on charcoal grill 4 to 6 inches from medium coals. Cook 8 to 10 minutes, or until chicken is fork-tender and juices run clear, turning once.

4. Meanwhile, in large bowl, combine lettuce and dressing; toss to coat. Arrange salad on 4 individual plates.

5. Cut each chicken breast half crosswise into slices; do not separate slices. Fan 1 chicken breast half over lettuce mixture on each plate. Top each salad with 2 tomato wedges.

Yield: 4 servings

Broiler Directions: 1. Prepare dressing as directed above. Lightly sprinkle both sides of each chicken breast half with herb blend. Place chicken on broiler pan.
2. Broil 4 to 6 inches from heat for 8 to 10 minutes, or until chicken is fork-tender and juices run clear, turning once. Continue as directed above.

Nutrition Information Per Serving

Serving Size: ¼ of Recipe • Calories 250 • Calories from Fat 100 • Total Fat 11 g
Saturated Fat 3 g • Cholesterol 75 mg • Sodium 210 mg • Dietary Fiber 4 g
Dietary Exchanges: 1 Vegetable, 4 Lean Meat

About Worcestershire Sauce

Worcestershire sauce, available on grocery shelves, gets its brown color and unmistakable flavor from an unlikely blend of ingredients that includes anchovies, molasses, sugar, vinegar, tamarind, onions, garlic, shallots and spices.

California Chicken Salad

Prep Time: 15 minutes

Salad
- **7 cups torn leaf lettuce**
- **7 cups torn romaine lettuce**
- **6 boneless, skinless chicken breast halves, cooked, cut into bite-sized pieces**
- **4 oz. Canadian bacon, sliced, cut into thin strips (1 cup)**
- **¾ cup sliced green onions**
- **2 medium tomatoes, chopped**

Vinaigrette
- **½ cup balsamic vinegar**
- **⅓ cup oil**
- **2 teaspoons Dijon mustard**
- **2 garlic cloves, minced**

1. In large bowl, combine all salad ingredients; mix well.
2. In small bowl, combine all vinaigrette ingredients; blend well. Just before serving, pour vinaigrette over salad; toss gently.

Yield: 10 (1⅔-cup) servings

Nutrition Information Per Serving

Serving Size: 1⅔ Cups • Calories 190 • Calories from Fat 90 • Total Fat 10 g
Saturated Fat 2 g • Cholesterol 50 mg • Sodium 230 mg • Dietary Fiber 2 g
Dietary Exchanges: 1 Vegetable, 2½ Lean Meat, ½ Fat

Recipe Fact

This West Coast–inspired main-dish salad gives a healthier twist to traditional chef's salads, which are heavy with fatty cold cuts and cheese.

About Balsamic Vinegar

Balsamic vinegar, a dark brown vinegar from Italy, gains its characteristic sweet, mellow flavor as it ages in oak barrels.

Cobb Salad

Prep Time: 45 minutes

1½ cups cubed cooked chicken

2 eggs, hard-cooked, coarsely chopped

6 slices bacon, crisply cooked, crumbled

4 cups torn salad greens

1 large tomato, chopped

¼ cup sliced green onions

1 medium avocado, peeled, sliced or cubed, tossed in lemon juice

4 oz. (1 cup) crumbled blue cheese

½ to 1 cup purchased fat-free or reduced-calorie thousand island salad dressing

On large serving platter or in 13 × 9-inch (3-quart) baking dish, arrange all ingredients except dressing in rows. Or, arrange ingredients on 6 individual plates. Serve salad with dressing or spoon dressing over each salad.

Yield: 6 servings

Nutrition Information Per Serving

Serving Size: ⅙ of Recipe • Calories 320 • Calories from Fat 160 • Total Fat 18 g
Saturated Fat 7 g • Cholesterol 120 mg • Sodium 850 mg • Dietary Fiber 4 g
Dietary Exchanges: 1 Starch, 1 Vegetable, 2 Lean Meat, 2½ Fat OR
1 Carbohydrate, 1 Vegetable, 2 Lean Meat, 2½ Fat

Recipe Fact

This famous salad is named for Bob Cobb, the proprietor of the former Brown Derby restaurant in Hollywood. He created the salad as a way to use up leftovers. The name is now commonly used to describe any chopped salad.

Kitchen Tip

To cut up an avocado, halve it from stem end to blossom end, cutting just deeply enough to reach the large pit. Gently pull the halves apart and remove the pit. Use a teaspoon or melon baller to scoop out flesh. Or, cut the avocado into slices and run a knife between the skin and the flesh, just as you would skin a slice of cantaloupe. Toss the cut pieces with lemon juice right away to prevent browning.

Cobb Salad

Chicken Broccoli Potato Salad

30 min. or less • editor's choice

Healthy Hint

A simple substitution of reduced-fat mayonnaise for the regular will cut the fat from 32 grams per serving to 8 grams and calories from 450 to 300. If you use nonfat mayonnaise, fat will be reduced to 6 grams, calories to 230.

Ingredient Substitution

To emphasize summery flavor, use 1½ teaspoons minced fresh oregano leaves instead of the dried.

Prep Time: 15 minutes

Dressing
¾ cup mayonnaise
2 tablespoons grated
   Parmesan cheese
½ teaspoon sugar
½ teaspoon dried oregano
   leaves
¼ teaspoon onion powder

Salad
2 cups diced cooked potatoes
2 cups frozen cut broccoli,
   cooked crisp-tender,
   drained
2 cups cubed cooked chicken
1 (2-oz.) jar diced pimiento,
   drained

1. In small jar with tight-fitting lid, combine all dressing ingredients; shake well.

2. In large bowl, combine all salad ingredients. Add dressing; stir gently to coat.

Yield: 5 (1-cup) servings

Nutrition Information Per Serving

Serving Size: 1 Cup • Calories 450 • Calories from Fat 290 • Total Fat 32 g
Saturated Fat 6 g • Cholesterol 70 mg • Sodium 310 mg • Dietary Fiber 3 g
Dietary Exchanges: 1 Starch, 1 Vegetable, 2 Lean Meat, 5 Fat OR
1 Carbohydrate, 1 Vegetable, 2 Lean Meat, 5 Fat

Chicken Broccoli Potato Salad

Fajita Chicken Salad

Prep Time: 30 minutes

2 (8-inch) flour tortillas

Salad
1 tablespoon oil
1 tablespoon red wine vinegar
1 teaspoon chopped fresh cilantro
1 teaspoon fresh lime juice
½ teaspoon sugar
⅛ teaspoon garlic powder
4 cups shredded leaf lettuce

Chicken
2 boneless, skinless chicken breast halves, thinly sliced
1 small onion, cut into thin wedges
1 medium red or green bell pepper, cut into $1 \times \frac{1}{4} \times \frac{1}{4}$-inch strips
½ teaspoon chili powder
½ teaspoon coarsely ground black pepper
¼ teaspoon cumin

1. Heat oven to 375°F. Cut tortillas into ¼-inch strips; cut strips into 2-inch pieces. Place in single layer on ungreased cookie sheet. Bake at 375°F. for 6 to 8 minutes, or until lightly browned and crisp.

2. Meanwhile, in small jar with tight-fitting lid, combine all salad ingredients except lettuce; shake well. In medium bowl, combine lettuce and dressing; toss gently to coat. Arrange on 4 individual plates.

3. Spray large skillet with nonstick cooking spray. Heat over medium-high heat until hot. Add all chicken ingredients; cook and stir 5 to 7 minutes, or until chicken is no longer pink and vegetables are tender. Place ¼ of warm chicken mixture on each salad; top with tortilla strips.

Yield: 4 servings

Nutrition Information Per Serving
Serving Size: ¼ of Recipe • Calories 200 • Calories from Fat 60 • Total Fat 7 g
Saturated Fat 1 g • Cholesterol 50 mg • Sodium 135 mg • Dietary Fiber 2 g
Dietary Exchanges: ½ Starch, 2 Vegetable, 2 Lean Meat OR
½ Carbohydrate, 2 Vegetable, 2 Lean Meat

Lemon Mint Chicken Salad

low-fat

Prep Time: 30 minutes
(Ready in 3 hours 30 minutes)

Salad
1 (16-oz.) pkg. uncooked bow tie pasta (farfalle)
6 cups cubed cooked chicken
4 cups seedless green or red grapes
4 cups cantaloupe cubes
3 cups thinly sliced celery
1 cup sliced green onions

½ cup reduced-calorie mayonnaise or salad dressing
1 to 2 tablespoons chopped fresh mint
1 tablespoon grated lemon peel
1½ teaspoons salt
½ teaspoon pepper

Dressing
2 (8-oz.) containers low-fat lemon yogurt

Garnish
¼ cup slivered almonds, toasted*

1. Cook pasta to desired doneness as directed on package. Drain; rinse with cold water. In very large bowl, combine all salad ingredients; mix well.
2. In medium bowl, combine all dressing ingredients; blend well. Add dressing to salad; mix well. Cover; refrigerate 3 hours to blend flavors. Just before serving, sprinkle with almonds.

Yield: 21 (1-cup) servings

*Tip: To toast almonds, spread evenly on cookie sheet; bake at 350°F. for 5 to 7 minutes, or until light golden brown, stirring occasionally. Or, spread almonds in thin layer in microwave-safe pie pan. Microwave on HIGH for 4 to 7 minutes, or until golden brown, stirring frequently.

Nutrition Information Per Serving
Serving Size: 1 Cup • Calories 250 • Calories from Fat 60 • Total Fat 7 g
Saturated Fat 2 g • Cholesterol 40 mg • Sodium 270 mg • Dietary Fiber 2 g
Dietary Exchanges: 1 Starch, 1 Fruit, 2 Lean Meat OR
2 Carbohydrate, 2 Lean Meat

Recipe Fact
This large-quantity recipe makes a wonderful buffet dish.

About Bow Tie Pasta
Bow tie pasta is called **farfalle** ("little butterflies") in Italian.

Make It Special
For a buffet, spoon the salad into a shallow rectangular or oval serving dish. Arrange a row of paper-thin lemon slices down the center or around the edges and accent with sprigs of fresh mint.

Easy Oriental Chicken Salad

Prep Time: 20 minutes
(Ready in 35 minutes)

¼ cup soy sauce
¼ cup water
2 boneless, skinless chicken breast halves, cut into thin crosswise strips
1 (8-oz.) can sliced water chestnuts, drained
1 cup julienne-cut (1 × ¼ × ¼-inch) carrots
½ cup diagonally sliced green onions
¼ cup sugar
½ cup oil
⅓ cup white wine vinegar
½ teaspoon ginger
1½ cups finely chopped red cabbage
1 cup chow mein noodles

1. In large skillet, bring soy sauce and water to a boil. Add chicken. Reduce heat; cover and simmer 5 to 8 minutes, or until chicken is no longer pink. Drain; cool 15 minutes.

2. In medium bowl, combine water chestnuts, carrots, green onions and chicken.

3. In small jar with tight-fitting lid, combine sugar, oil, vinegar and ginger; shake well. Pour over salad; toss to coat. Just before serving, add cabbage and chow mein noodles to salad; toss gently.

Yield: 4 (1½-cup) servings

Nutrition Information Per Serving

Serving Size: 1½ Cups • Calories 480 • Calories from Fat 290 • Total Fat 32 g
Saturated Fat 4 g • Cholesterol 35 mg • Sodium 360 mg • Dietary Fiber 3 g
Dietary Exchanges: 1 Starch, 1 Fruit, 2 Lean Meat, 5½ Fat OR
2 Carbohydrate, 2 Lean Meat, 5½ Fat

Kitchen Tip

To julienne the carrots (cut into thin strips), trim the root and stem ends. Slice the carrots lengthwise into thin (about ¼-inch-thick) planks. Stack the planks and cut them again into long, thin pieces about the thickness of a wooden matchstick. Finally, cut the strips crosswise into pieces about 1 inch long.

Ingredient Substitution

Chinese cabbage can replace the red cabbage.

Easy Oriental Chicken Salad

Grilled Chicken Satay Salad

Prep Time: 35 minutes
(Ready in 1 hour 35 minutes)

Recipe Fact

Satay, claimed by several Asian countries as their national dish, is closely associated with Indonesian cooking. It refers to grilled strips of meat (often skewered), usually served with a peanut sauce.

Kitchen Tip

To remove the skin of a garlic clove easily, press the clove firmly with the broad side of a chef's knife. Slice off the ends and the skin will pop right off.

Recipe Variation

For a delicious appetizer, pound the raw chicken breast, cut it into strips and thread the pieces onto wooden skewers that have been soaked in water for 30 minutes to prevent scorching. Grill the skewers and heap them on a serving platter surrounding a dish of the peanut dressing.

1 (7- or 8-inch) flour tortilla, halved, cut into 1/8- to 1/4-inch strips

1 tablespoon soy sauce
1/2 teaspoon minced gingerroot
1 garlic clove, minced

Dressing
1/3 cup rice vinegar or cider vinegar
1/4 cup creamy peanut butter
3 tablespoons finely chopped peanuts
2 tablespoons sugar
2 tablespoons oil
2 tablespoons sesame oil

Salad
4 boneless, skinless chicken breast halves
6 cups torn mixed salad greens
1 cup finely shredded red cabbage
1/3 cup shredded carrot
1/4 cup chopped fresh cilantro or fresh parsley

1. Heat oven to 350°F. Arrange tortilla strips in single layer on ungreased cookie sheet. Bake at 350°F. for 7 to 11 minutes, or until lightly browned.

2. Meanwhile, in small bowl, combine all dressing ingredients; blend with wire whisk until smooth and creamy. Place chicken in resealable plastic bag; add 3 tablespoons of the dressing. Seal bag; turn to coat. Refrigerate 1 to 2 hours. Refrigerate remaining dressing. In large bowl, combine remaining salad ingredients; toss. Cover; refrigerate.

3. Heat grill. When ready to grill, oil grill rack. Place chicken on gas grill over medium heat or on charcoal grill 4 to 6 inches from medium coals. Cook 10 to 15 minutes, or until chicken is fork-tender and juices run clear, turning once.

4. Cut chicken into strips. Add chicken and remaining refrigerated dressing to salad; toss to coat. Arrange salad on 6 individual plates; sprinkle with tortilla strips.

Yield: 6 servings

Grilled Chicken Satay Salad

Nutrition Information Per Serving

Serving Size: ⅙ of Recipe • Calories 330 • Calories from Fat 180 • Total Fat 20 g
Saturated Fat 3 g • Cholesterol 45 mg • Sodium 330 mg • Dietary Fiber 2 g
Dietary Exchanges: ½ Starch, 1 Vegetable, 3 Lean Meat, 2 Fat OR
½ Carbohydrate, 1 Vegetable, 3 Lean Meat, 2 Fat

Grilled Chicken Taco Salad

Prep Time: 30 minutes

Dressing
⅓ cup purchased reduced-calorie French salad dressing
⅓ cup purchased thick and chunky salsa
¼ cup sliced green onions

Salad
4 boneless, skinless chicken breast halves
½ teaspoon chili powder
¼ teaspoon garlic powder
4 cups shredded lettuce
2 medium tomatoes, chopped
4 oz. (1 cup) shredded reduced-fat Cheddar cheese
½ cup (1 oz.) tortilla chips
¼ cup nonfat sour cream

Grill Directions: 1. In small bowl, combine all dressing ingredients; blend well. Refrigerate until serving time.
2. Heat grill. Place 1 chicken breast half between 2 pieces of plastic wrap or waxed paper. Working from center, gently pound chicken with flat side of meat mallet or rolling pin until about ¼ inch thick; remove wrap. Repeat with remaining chicken breast halves. Sprinkle chicken with chili powder and garlic powder.
3. When ready to grill, place chicken on gas grill over medium heat or on charcoal grill 4 to 6 inches from medium-high coals. Cook 8 to 10 minutes, or until chicken is fork-tender and juices run clear, turning once.
4. Arrange lettuce, tomatoes and cheese on 4 individual plates. Cut chicken crosswise into slices; place over lettuce mixture. Arrange tortilla chips around edge of each plate. Drizzle dressing over each salad; top with sour cream.

Yield: 4 servings

Broiler Directions: 1. Prepare recipe as directed above. Place chicken on broiler pan.

2. Broil 4 to 6 inches from heat for 8 to 10 minutes, or until chicken is fork-tender and juices run clear, turning once. Continue as directed above.

Nutrition Information Per Serving

Serving Size: ¼ of Recipe • Calories 340 • Calories from Fat 110 • Total Fat 12 g
Saturated Fat 5 g • Cholesterol 95 mg • Sodium 710 mg • Dietary Fiber 3 g
Dietary Exchanges: ½ Starch, 2 Vegetable, 4½ Lean Meat OR
½ Carbohydrate, 2 Vegetable, 4½ Lean Meat

Grilled Chicken Taco Salad

Chicken Salad Italiana

About Bibb Lettuce

Bibb lettuce, also called butterhead lettuce, is a small, loosely formed head with tender, light green leaves. Use it as you would other soft-leaf lettuces.

About Italian Seasoning

Dried Italian seasoning is an herb mix that may contain any or all of the following: marjoram, oregano, thyme, rosemary, savory, sage and basil.

Kitchen Tip

To prepare asparagus, snap off the bottom ends of the stalks where they break naturally. If the stalks are fat and the skin seems tough, peel the base of the stalk with a vegetable peeler or sharp knife.

⅓ cup balsamic vinegar*
2 tablespoons water
2 teaspoons dried Italian seasoning
4 boneless, skinless chicken breast halves
1 tablespoon oil
½ teaspoon sugar

½ lb. asparagus
8 cups torn Bibb lettuce
1 (15-oz.) can garbanzo beans, drained, rinsed
1 small red onion, sliced, separated into rings
1 medium tomato, cut into 8 wedges

Grill Directions: 1. Heat grill. In small bowl, combine vinegar, water and Italian seasoning; mix well. Place 2 to 3 tablespoons vinegar mixture in medium bowl. Add chicken; toss to coat. Let stand 5 to 10 minutes at room temperature to marinate. To prepare dressing, add oil and sugar to remaining vinegar mixture in small bowl; mix well. Set aside.

2. Place 1 chicken breast half between 2 pieces of plastic wrap or waxed paper. Working from center, gently pound chicken with flat side of meat mallet or rolling pin until about ¼ inch thick; remove wrap. Repeat with remaining chicken breast halves.

3. When ready to grill, remove chicken from marinade; discard marinade. Place chicken on gas grill over medium heat or on charcoal grill 4 to 6 inches from medium coals. Cook 8 to 10 minutes, or until chicken is fork-tender and juices run clear, turning once.

4. Meanwhile, place asparagus in large skillet; add ½ inch water. Bring to a boil. Reduce heat; cover and simmer 2 to 4 minutes, or until asparagus is bright green and crisp-tender.

5. Arrange lettuce on 4 individual plates; sprinkle each with garbanzo beans. Slice each chicken breast half crosswise into slices; do not separate slices. Fan chicken slices; arrange 1 breast half on lettuce mixture on each plate.

Arrange steamed asparagus, onion rings and tomato wedges around chicken. Serve with dressing.

Yield: 4 servings

Broiler Directions: 1. Marinate chicken and prepare dressing as directed above. Place chicken on broiler pan. Broil 4 to 6 inches from heat for 8 to 10 minutes, or until chicken is fork-tender and juices run clear, turning once. **2.** Steam asparagus and assemble salad as directed above.

*Tip: To substitute for balsamic vinegar, use ¼ cup cider vinegar and 2 tablespoons brown sugar; mix well.

Nutrition Information Per Serving

Serving Size: ¼ of Recipe • Calories 320 • Calories from Fat 80 • Total Fat 9 g
Saturated Fat 2 g • Cholesterol 75 mg • Sodium 230 mg • Dietary Fiber 7 g
Dietary Exchanges: 1 Starch, 2 Vegetable, 4 Very Lean Meat, 1 Fat OR
1 Carbohydrate, 2 Vegetable, 4 Very Lean Meat, 1 Fat

Couscous Chicken Salad

Prep Time: 20 minutes
(Ready in 1 hour 40 minutes)

About Couscous

Couscous, a North African staple pasta that resembles grain, is available in a quick-to-prepare version that cooks in just 5 minutes.

Ingredient Substitution

Use rice in place of the couscous, and cook according to package directions.

Salad

1 cup uncooked couscous
2 cups shredded cooked chicken
1 cup chopped green bell pepper
1 cup sliced celery
½ cup shredded carrot
2 green onions, sliced

Dressing

⅓ cup orange juice
⅓ cup oil
¼ cup chopped fresh parsley
2 tablespoons lemon juice
2 tablespoons soy sauce
1 teaspoon finely chopped gingerroot or ¼ teaspoon ground ginger
Dash salt
⅛ teaspoon pepper

1. Cook couscous as directed on package. Uncover; cool 20 minutes.

2. In large bowl, combine couscous and all remaining salad ingredients; toss gently.

3. In small jar with tight-fitting lid, combine all dressing ingredients; shake well. Pour dressing over salad; toss gently. Cover; refrigerate 1 to 2 hours to blend flavors. If desired, serve on lettuce-lined plates.

Yield: 7 (1-cup) servings

Nutrition Information Per Serving

Serving Size: 1 Cup • Calories 290 • Calories from Fat 130 • Total Fat 14 g
Saturated Fat 2 g • Cholesterol 35 mg • Sodium 370 mg • Dietary Fiber 2 g
Dietary Exchanges: 1 Starch, 2 Vegetable, 1½ Lean Meat, 2 Fat OR
1 Carbohydrate, 2 Vegetable, 1½ Lean Meat, 2 Fat

Pacific Coast Chicken Salad

Prep Time: 20 minutes
(Ready in 1 hour 20 minutes)

Dressing
⅓ cup orange juice
2 tablespoons oil
1 tablespoon white wine
    vinegar
1 tablespoon honey
1 teaspoon celery seed, if
    desired
⅛ teaspoon hot pepper sauce

Salad
3 cups torn iceberg lettuce
2 cups torn spinach
2 cups cubed cooked chicken
    breasts
2 medium oranges, peeled,
    sectioned
1 pink grapefruit, peeled,
    sectioned
1 ripe medium avocado,
    peeled, cubed
¼ cup slivered almonds,
    toasted*

1. In small jar with tight-fitting lid, combine all dressing ingredients; shake well. Refrigerate 1 to 2 hours to blend flavors.

2. In large bowl, combine all salad ingredients except almonds; toss gently. When ready to serve, shake dressing. Pour over salad; toss gently to coat. Top with almonds.

Yield: 6 (2-cup) servings

*Tip: To toast almonds, spread on cookie sheet; bake at 350°F. for 5 to 7 minutes, or until golden brown, stirring occasionally. Or, spread almonds in thin layer in microwave-safe pie pan. Microwave on HIGH for 4 to 7 minutes, or until golden brown, stirring frequently.

Nutrition Information Per Serving
Serving Size: 2 Cups • Calories 270 • Calories from Fat 130 • Total Fat 14 g
Saturated Fat 2 g • Cholesterol 40 mg • Sodium 55 mg • Dietary Fiber 5 g
Dietary Exchanges: 1 Fruit, 1 Vegetable, 2 Lean Meat, 1½ Fat OR
1 Carbohydrate, 1 Vegetable, 2 Lean Meat, 1½ Fat

Kitchen Tip

To remove the core from iceberg lettuce easily, bang the whole head, core end down, firmly on a table or counter. It will be easy to pry out the core with your fingers. Tear the rinsed and drained lettuce into pieces with your fingers rather than cutting it with a knife to avoid bruising and discoloring the leaves.

Kitchen Tip

To prepare an orange for a salad, pare the skin off the entire orange with a sharp knife, cutting just deeply enough to expose the flesh. Make V-shaped cuts just along the inside of each dividing membrane to release the flesh without including the membrane. Work over a bowl to catch the juices as you cut and incorporate them into the dressing.

Papaya and Chicken Salad

About Papayas

A papaya tree grows from seed to the height of 20 feet within 18 months. To prepare the fruit, cut it in half and scoop out the center mass of pulp and brown-black seeds. Cut the fruit into slices, then run a knife between the flesh and the skin to peel.

Make It Special

Lime has a special affinity for papaya and cantaloupe. Garnish the salad with shredded or grated lime zest or with slices or wedges of lime.

Prep Time: 20 minutes

1 large papaya or 1 small cantaloupe
1 tablespoon lime juice
2 cups cubed cooked chicken
6 oz. (1½ cups) fresh pea pods, cut into thirds
¼ cup chopped green onions
½ cup reduced-calorie or regular mayonnaise
2 tablespoons lime juice
½ teaspoon salt
¼ teaspoon pepper
4 leaves leaf lettuce
4 teaspoons sesame seed, toasted*

1. Quarter, seed and peel papaya; sprinkle with 1 tablespoon lime juice. In medium bowl, combine chicken, pea pods and green onions.
2. In small bowl, combine mayonnaise, 2 tablespoons lime juice, salt and pepper; blend well. Spoon mayonnaise mixture over chicken mixture; toss gently.
3. Arrange lettuce on 4 individual plates; top with papaya. Spoon ¼ of chicken mixture over each papaya quarter; sprinkle each with sesame seed.

Yield: 4 servings

*Tip: To toast sesame seed, place seed in skillet. Stir over medium heat for 1 to 2 minutes, or until light golden brown.

Nutrition Information Per Serving

Serving Size: ¼ of Recipe • Calories 310 • Calories from Fat 140 • Total Fat 16 g
Saturated Fat 4 g • Cholesterol 70 mg • Sodium 550 mg • Dietary Fiber 4 g
Dietary Exchanges: ½ Fruit, 2 Vegetable, 3 Lean Meat, 1½ Fat OR
½ Carbohydrate, 2 Vegetable, 3 Lean Meat, 1½ Fat

Waldorf Chicken Salad

Prep Time: 20 minutes

Dressing
1 (8-oz.) container low-fat plain
    yogurt
2 tablespoons honey
¼ teaspoon ginger

Salad
2 cups cubed cooked chicken
1 cup chopped apple

1 cup seedless red grapes,
    halved
½ cup thinly sliced celery
½ cup raisins
4 leaves lettuce, if desired
2 tablespoons chopped
    walnuts

1. In small bowl, combine all dressing ingredients; blend well.

2. In large bowl, combine all salad ingredients except lettuce and walnuts. Pour dressing over salad; toss gently to coat. Arrange lettuce on 4 individual plates. Spoon salad over lettuce; sprinkle with walnuts.

Yield: 4 servings

Nutrition Information Per Serving
Serving Size: ¼ of Recipe • Calories 350 • Calories from Fat 80 • Total Fat 9 g
Saturated Fat 2 g • Cholesterol 65 mg • Sodium 115 mg • Dietary Fiber 3 g
Dietary Exchanges: 2½ Fruit, 3½ Lean Meat OR 2½ Carbohydrate, 3½ Lean Meat

---

Recipe Fact

A classic Waldorf salad combines chopped apple, celery and walnuts in a mayonnaise-based dressing. The cubed chicken makes it a heartier main-dish salad.

Recipe Variation

For a winter meal, make the salad without the chicken and serve it alongside roasted poultry instead.

Make It Special

Use a combination of unpeeled, chopped red and green apples for visual contrast. Granny Smith and Red Delicious apples or other firm varieties work especially well.

Summer Fruit and Chicken Salad

Prep Time: 15 minutes

Dressing
½ cup low-fat raspberry yogurt
¼ cup mayonnaise or salad dressing
2 tablespoons honey

Salad
4 leaves leaf lettuce
½ lb. thinly sliced cooked chicken
½ medium cantaloupe, seeds removed, peeled, cut into very thin slices
1 cup fresh raspberries
½ cup fresh blueberries

1. In small bowl, combine all dressing ingredients; blend well. Refrigerate until serving time.
2. To serve, arrange lettuce on large platter or on 4 individual plates. Arrange chicken, cantaloupe, raspberries and blueberries over lettuce. Drizzle with dressing.

Yield: 4 servings

Nutrition Information Per Serving
Serving Size: ¼ of Recipe • Calories 300 • Calories from Fat 120 • Total Fat 13 g
Saturated Fat 2 g • Cholesterol 35 mg • Sodium 590 mg • Dietary Fiber 4 g
Dietary Exchanges: 2 Fruit, 2 Lean Meat, 1½ Fat OR
2 Carbohydrate, 2 Lean Meat, 1½ Fat

Summer Fruit and Chicken Salad

Grilled Chicken and Spinach Salad with Orange Dressing

Prep Time: 25 minutes

1 (10-oz.) pkg. fresh prewashed spinach, torn
½ cup orange juice
3 tablespoons brown sugar
3 tablespoons vinegar
1 teaspoon grated orange peel
⅛ teaspoon salt
2 medium shallots, minced
4 boneless, skinless chicken breast halves
¼ teaspoon black and red pepper blend or black pepper
6 orange slices, halved
1½ cups fresh strawberry halves

Grill Directions: 1. Heat grill. Place spinach in large bowl. In small saucepan, combine orange juice, brown sugar, vinegar, orange peel, salt and shallots; mix well. Bring to a boil over medium heat, stirring occasionally. Immediately pour over spinach; toss to combine. Arrange on 4 individual plates.

2. Place 1 chicken breast half between 2 pieces of plastic wrap or waxed paper. Working from center, gently pound chicken with flat side of meat mallet or rolling pin until about ¼ inch thick; remove wrap. Repeat with remaining chicken breast halves.

3. When ready to grill, sprinkle half of pepper blend on tops of chicken breast halves. Place chicken, peppered side down, on gas grill over medium heat or on charcoal grill 4 to 6 inches from medium coals. Cook 5 minutes. Sprinkle chicken with remaining pepper blend; turn chicken. Cook an additional 3 to 5 minutes, or until chicken is fork-tender and juices run clear.

4. Cut chicken breasts crosswise into slices; do not separate slices. Fan 1 chicken breast half over spinach mixture on each plate. Arrange orange slices and straw-berries around chicken.

Yield: 4 servings

Broiler Directions: 1. Prepare spinach mixture as directed above. Sprinkle half of pepper blend on tops of chicken breast halves. Place chicken, peppered side up, on broiler pan. Broil 4 to 6 inches from heat for 5 minutes. **2.** Turn chicken; sprinkle with remaining pepper blend. Broil an additional 3 to 5 minutes, or until chicken is fork-tender and juices run clear. Continue as directed above.

Nutrition Information Per Serving

Serving Size: ¼ of Recipe • Calories 260 • Calories from Fat 35 • Total Fat 4 g
Saturated Fat 1 g • Cholesterol 75 mg • Sodium 190 mg • Dietary Fiber 4 g
Dietary Exchanges: 1½ Fruit, 1 Vegetable, 4 Very Lean Meat OR
1½ Carbohydrate, 1 Vegetable, 4 Very Lean Meat

Grilled Chicken and Spinach Salad with Orange Dressing

What's the occasion? Turn the page to find a chicken sandwich to match it. Choose from quick-fix versions just right for popping into a brown bag or the picnic basket, delicate make-ahead offerings well

Sandwiches

suited to a formal reception, or hot pita- or taco-wrapped entrees that are perfect for a satisfying supper. Hot or cold, the choices abound.

Sandwiches

Previous page: Mandarin Chicken Pockets page 67

Mandarin Chicken Pockets

30 min. or less • low-fat

Prep Time: 15 minutes

1 cup chopped cooked chicken
1 (11-oz.) can mandarin orange segments, well drained
½ cup chopped celery
¼ cup sliced almonds, if desired
2 green onions, sliced

3 tablespoons mayonnaise or salad dressing
¼ teaspoon salt
Dash pepper
3 (6-inch) pita (pocket) breads, cut in half
6 lettuce leaves

1. In medium bowl, combine all ingredients except pita breads and lettuce leaves; mix well.
2. Line each pita bread half with lettuce leaf; fill with ⅓ cup chicken mixture.

Yield: 6 sandwiches

Nutrition Information Per Serving
Serving Size: 1 Sandwich • Calories 230 • Calories from Fat 90 • Total Fat 10 g
Saturated Fat 2 g • Cholesterol 25 mg • Sodium 320 mg • Dietary Fiber 2 g
Dietary Exchanges: 1 Starch, ½ Fruit, 1 Lean Meat, 1½ Fat OR
1½ Carbohydrate, 1 Lean Meat, 1½ Fat

Ingredient Substitution

Substitute one cup of halved seedless grapes for the mandarin orange segments.

Make-Ahead Tip

Prepare the filling up to a day ahead and refrigerate it. Add the almonds and lettuce just before serving time to prevent them from getting soggy.

Bacon Cheddar Chicken Fillet Melt

Prep Time: 30 minutes

About Pumpernickel Bread

Pumpernickel bread, of German origin, gets its brown color and depth of flavor from molasses.

Kitchen Tip

Cook the bacon in the microwave oven sandwiched between layers of white microwave-safe paper towels. Instead of browning the onion and chicken in the bacon fat, spritz the skillet with nonfat cooking spray.

Healthy Hint

Cut 7 grams of fat per serving by substituting reduced-fat Cheddar for regular and using one slice of bacon per sandwich instead of two.

4 boneless, skinless chicken breast halves
8 slices bacon
1 small red onion, sliced
4 slices pumpernickel bread, toasted

4 teaspoons steak sauce
4 oz. (1 cup) shredded Cheddar cheese

1. Place 1 chicken breast half between 2 pieces of plastic wrap or waxed paper. Working from center, gently pound chicken with flat side of meat mallet or rolling pin until about ¼ inch thick; remove wrap. Repeat with remaining chicken breast halves.

2. Cook bacon in large skillet over medium heat until crisp. Remove bacon; drain on paper towels. Reserve 1 tablespoon drippings in skillet. Add onion to drippings; cook and stir 2 to 4 minutes, or until tender. Remove onion from skillet. Add chicken to skillet; cook 6 to 8 minutes on each side, or until lightly browned and juices run clear.

3. Place toasted bread slices on cookie sheet; spread each slice with 1 teaspoon steak sauce. Top with chicken, bacon slices, onion and cheese. Broil 4 to 6 inches from heat for 1 to 2 minutes, or until cheese is melted.

Yield: 4 sandwiches

Nutrition Information Per Serving

Serving Size: 1 Sandwich • Calories 440 • Calories from Fat 210 • Total Fat 23 g
Saturated Fat 10 g • Cholesterol 115 mg • Sodium 760 mg • Dietary Fiber 2 g
Dietary Exchanges: 1 Starch, 5 Lean Meat, 2 Fat OR
1 Carbohydrate, 5 Lean Meat, 2 Fat

Bacon Cheddar Chicken Fillet Melt

Cashew Chicken Sandwich Loaf

Recipe Fact

This savory sandwich, with its cream cheese "frosting," looks like a piece of cake.

Kitchen Tip

To soften the cream cheese, unwrap it, place it in a glass microwave-safe bowl and heat it in the microwave oven for about a minute or two, until the cheese is soft enough to be easily thinned with milk.

Healthy Hint

Slash the fat by using the nonfat versions of mayonnaise and cream cheese. Thin the cream cheese with skim milk instead of half-and-half. Total savings: 21 grams fat per portion.

Prep Time: 30 minutes
(Ready in 2 hours 30 minutes)

1 (1-lb.) unsliced loaf whole wheat or white sandwich bread, crusts removed*
½ cup margarine or butter, softened

½ cup chopped cashews
½ cup mayonnaise or salad dressing
¼ teaspoon salt
⅛ teaspoon pepper

Filling
2½ cups finely chopped cooked chicken
½ cup finely chopped celery
2 tablespoons finely chopped onion

Topping
2 (8-oz.) pkg. cream cheese, softened
½ cup half-and-half

1. Cut loaf lengthwise into 4 slices. Spread 3 slices with margarine.
2. In small bowl, combine all filling ingredients; mix well. Spread ⅓ of filling over margarine on each slice of bread. Stack slices on serving plate, placing plain slice on top.
3. In large bowl, combine cream cheese and half-and-half; mix well. Spread over sides and top of loaf. Cover carefully with plastic wrap; refrigerate at least 2 hours.
4. Just before serving, garnish with chopped parsley and cashews, if desired. Store in refrigerator.

Yield: 12 servings

*Tip: Sandwich loaf can be made with alternating white and whole wheat slices; use remaining slices for a second sandwich loaf or other party sandwiches.

Nutrition Information Per Serving
Serving Size: ¹⁄₁₂ of Recipe • Calories 440 • Calories from Fat 320• Total Fat 35 g
Saturated Fat 13 g • Cholesterol 75 mg • Sodium 490 mg • Dietary Fiber 2 g
Dietary Exchanges: 1 Starch, 1½ Lean Meat, 6 Fat OR
1 Carbohydrate, 1½ Lean Meat, 6 Fat

Southwest Burrito Burgers

Prep Time: 30 minutes

1 lb. ground chicken
½ cup finely crushed tortilla
  chips or corn chips
¼ cup purchased salsa
4 (10-inch) flour tortillas

1 cup shredded lettuce
½ cup purchased guacamole
2 oz. (½ cup) shredded taco-
  flavored Cheddar cheese
½ cup purchased salsa

Grill Directions: 1. Heat grill. In medium bowl, combine ground chicken, tortilla chips and ¼ cup salsa; mix well. Shape mixture into four 4-inch-long oval patties. Wrap tortillas in 24 × 12-inch piece of heavy-duty foil; set aside.
2. When ready to grill, place patties on gas grill over medium-high heat or on charcoal grill 4 to 6 inches from medium-high coals. Cook 10 to 15 minutes, or until no longer pink in center, turning once. During last 1 to 2 minutes of cooking, place foil packet on grill. Heat until tortillas are softened.
3. Place lettuce in center of each tortilla; top each with burger, guacamole and cheese. Fold ends of tortilla toward center; overlap sides to cover burger. Serve with ½ cup salsa.

Yield: 4 sandwiches

Broiler Directions: 1. Prepare patties and foil packet as directed above. Place patties on broiler pan.
2. Broil 4 to 6 inches from heat for 10 to 15 minutes, or until no longer pink in center, turning once. During last 1 to 2 minutes of cooking, place foil packet on broiler pan. Heat until tortillas are softened. Continue as directed above.

About Salsa

Purchased salsa varies as to its ingredients but usually includes tomatoes, onion, chile peppers and cilantro; the texture can range from quite smooth to distinctively chunky.

About Guacamole

To make your own guacamole, mash the flesh of a ripe avocado together with lemon or lime juice, minced onion and diced jalapeños or hot pepper sauce. Mash it with a fork for a chunky texture or process it in a blender or food processor for a smoother dip.

Kitchen Tip

Crush the tortilla chips in a heavy plastic bag with a rolling pin or in a food processor with a metal blade.

Nutrition Information Per Serving

Serving Size: 1 Sandwich • Calories 450 • Calories from Fat 180 • Total Fat 20 g
Saturated Fat 8 g • Cholesterol 55 mg • Sodium 1200 mg • Dietary Fiber 4 g
Dietary Exchanges: 3 Starch, 2 Medium-Fat Meat, 1 Fat OR
3 Carbohydrate, 2 Medium-Fat Meat, 1 Fat

Chicken and Apricot Bagel Sandwiches

Prep time: 15 minutes

1 (5-oz.) can chunk white chicken breast in water, drained
⅓ cup chopped dried apricots
¼ cup chopped celery
2 tablespoons sliced green onions

2 teaspoons shelled sunflower seeds
Dash pepper
¼ cup fat-free mayonnaise or salad dressing
4 bagels, split

In small bowl, combine all ingredients except bagels; mix well. Fill each bagel with about ⅓ cup chicken mixture.

Yield: 4 sandwiches

Nutrition Information Per Serving

Serving Size: 1 Sandwich • Calories 290 • Calories from Fat 25 • Total Fat 3 g
Saturated Fat 0 g • Cholesterol 15 mg • Sodium 660 mg • Dietary Fiber 3 g
Dietary Exchanges: 2 Starch, 1 Fruit, 1½ Lean Meat OR
3 Carbohydrate, 1½ Lean Meat

Chicken and Apricot Bagel Sandwiches

Chicken Burgers with Cucumber Relish

Recipe Fact

The cucumber relish, made tangy with vinegar, also makes a fine accompaniment for grilled steak or fish.

About Ground Chicken

Ground chicken, an increasingly popular alternative to ground beef, is as versatile as hamburger but less fatty, and its mild flavor makes it a good foil for a wide range of seasonings. Ground chicken **breast** is even leaner. It has 3 grams of fat per 3 ounces cooked, compared to about 7.5 grams for ground chicken and 15 grams for 80% lean ground beef.

Prep Time: 35 minutes

Relish
- 1 medium cucumber, seeded, shredded
- ¼ cup chopped red or green bell pepper
- 2 tablespoons finely chopped onion
- 2 tablespoons mayonnaise or salad dressing
- 1 tablespoon vinegar
- 1 teaspoon chopped fresh dill or ¼ teaspoon dried dill weed
- ¼ teaspoon salt
- ⅛ teaspoon pepper

Burgers
- 1 lb. ground chicken
- ¼ cup Italian-style bread crumbs
- 2 tablespoons nonfat plain yogurt
- 2 teaspoons prepared horseradish
- 6 burger buns, split
- 6 leaves lettuce

Grill Directions: 1. In small bowl, combine all relish ingredients. Cover; refrigerate while preparing burgers. **2.** Heat grill. In large bowl, combine ground chicken, bread crumbs, yogurt and horseradish; mix well. Shape mixture into 6 patties. When ready to grill, place patties on gas grill over medium heat or on charcoal grill 4 to 6 inches from medium coals. Cook 8 to 12 minutes, or until no longer pink in center, turning once.
3. Toast burger buns on grill, cut side down, during last few minutes of cooking time. Place lettuce leaf on bottom half of each bun; top each with burger, relish and top half of bun.

Yield: 6 burgers

Broiler Directions: 1. Prepare relish and patties as directed above. Place patties on broiler pan.
2. Broil 4 to 6 inches from heat for 8 to 12 minutes, or until no longer pink in center, turning once. Toast burger

buns, cut side up, during last few minutes of cooking time. Serve burgers as directed above.

Nutrition Information Per Serving

Serving Size: 1 Burger • Calories 290 • Calories from Fat 120 • Total Fat 13 g
Saturated Fat 3 g • Cholesterol 45 mg • Sodium 500 mg • Dietary Fiber 1 g
Dietary Exchanges: 2 Starch, 1½ Lean Meat, 1½ Fat OR
2 Carbohydrate, 1½ Lean Meat, 1½ Fat

Chicken Muffuletta

30 min. or less

Prep Time: 10 minutes

1 round loaf Italian or
    sourdough bread, cut in
    half lengthwise
¼ cup soft cream cheese with
    olives and pimiento
3 leaves lettuce

4 oz. thinly sliced cooked
    chicken
1 cup drained pickled mixed
    vegetables, coarsely
    chopped*
4 oz. thinly sliced provolone
    cheese

1. Spread cut sides of bread halves with cream cheese. Layer bottom half of bread with lettuce, chicken, vegetables and cheese. Cover with top half of bread.
2. To serve, cut into wedges. If desired, secure each wedge with skewer or pick.

Yield: 6 servings

*Tip: Jars of pickled mixed vegetables can be found in the pickle section of most supermarkets.

Nutrition Information Per Serving

Serving Size: ⅙ of Recipe • Calories 330 • Calories from Fat 100 • Total Fat 11 g
Saturated Fat 6 g • Cholesterol 30 mg • Sodium 1090 mg • Dietary Fiber 3 g
Dietary Exchanges: 2½ Starch, 1 Vegetable, 1 Medium-Fat Meat, 1 Fat OR
2½ Carbohydrate, 1 Vegetable, 1 Medium-Fat Meat, 1 Fat

Recipe Fact

Originally from New Orleans, the muffuletta sandwich traditionally consists of an assortment of meats and cheeses and a tangy olive dressing.

Healthy Hint

Save 2 grams fat per serving by using reduced-fat cream cheese instead of regular.

Chicken and Pepper Sandwiches

Prep Time: 30 minutes

About Poblano Chiles

The poblano chile pepper is triangle or heart-shaped, about 2½ to 3 inches across at its widest part and 4 to 5 inches long. It's dark green in color—sometimes almost black—and ranges from mild to hot in flavor. Because of its large shape, it's a good choice for stuffing.

Recipe Variation

Instead of spooning the chicken mixture into rolls, serve it on a bed of rice pilaf or buttered noodles.

4 boneless, skinless chicken breast halves
½ teaspoon salt
½ teaspoon dried oregano leaves
¼ teaspoon pepper
1 tablespoon oil
1 poblano chile pepper or medium green bell pepper, seeded, cut into strips
1 medium onion, sliced, separated into rings
¾ cup refried beans
4 kaiser rolls, split
4 teaspoons margarine or butter
1 medium tomato, sliced
4 leaves lettuce

1. Place 1 chicken breast half between 2 pieces of plastic wrap or waxed paper. Working from center, gently pound chicken with flat side of meat mallet or rolling pin until about ¼ inch thick; remove wrap. Repeat with remaining chicken breast halves. Sprinkle chicken with salt, oregano and pepper.
2. Heat oil in large skillet over medium-high heat until hot. Add chicken; cook 6 to 8 minutes on each side, or until lightly browned and juices run clear. Remove from skillet; cover to keep warm.
3. In same skillet, cook chile pepper and onion 5 to 7 minutes, or until chile pepper is crisp-tender, stirring occasionally. Meanwhile, in medium saucepan, heat refried beans as directed on can.
4. Remove chile pepper mixture from skillet; keep warm. Heat same skillet over medium-high heat. Spread cut sides of rolls with margarine. Place rolls, margarine side down, in hot skillet. Cook 1 to 2 minutes, or until golden brown.

5. To assemble sandwiches, place 2 to 3 tablespoons of the refried beans on bottom half of each bun. Top with chicken breast half, pepper mixture, tomato and lettuce; cover with top half of rolls.

Yield: 4 sandwiches

Nutrition Information Per Serving

Serving Size: 1 Sandwich • Calories 440 • Calories from Fat 120 • Total Fat 13 g
Saturated Fat 3 g • Cholesterol 75 mg • Sodium 890 mg • Dietary Fiber 5 g
Dietary Exchanges: 3 Starch, 4 Lean Meat OR 3 Carbohydrate, 4 Lean Meat

Chicken and Pepper Sandwiches

Chicken Swisswiches

Ingredient Substitution

Try 2 cups of tender-cooked broccoli florets instead of the asparagus.

Recipe Variation

Serve the chicken salad cold on a bed of torn lettuce, with bread on the side.

Prep Time: 20 minutes

¼ cup margarine or butter, softened
10 slices white bread
1½ cups cubed cooked chicken
2 oz. (½ cup) shredded Swiss cheese

¼ cup chopped celery
⅓ cup mayonnaise or salad dressing
1 (10½-oz.) can cut asparagus spears, drained, or 2 cups cooked fresh asparagus

1. Spread margarine on' 1 side of each bread slice. In small bowl, combine chicken, cheese, celery and mayonnaise; mix well. Gently stir in asparagus.

2. To assemble sandwiches, spread chicken mixture on unbuttered side of 5 bread slices. Top with remaining bread slices, buttered side up.

3. Heat griddle or large skillet to 375°F. Cook sandwiches 2 to 3 minutes on each side, or until golden brown and cheese is melted.

Yield: 5 sandwiches

Nutrition Information Per Serving

Serving Size: 1 Sandwich • Calories 450 • Calories from Fat 260 • Total Fat 29 g
Saturated Fat 7 g • Cholesterol 55 mg • Sodium 670 mg • Dietary Fiber 2 g
Dietary Exchanges: 2 Starch, 2 Lean Meat, 4½ Fat OR
2 Carbohydrate, 2 Lean Meat, 4½ Fat

Hot Sourdough Chicken Sandwiches

Prep Time: 15 minutes

⅓ cup reduced-calorie
    mayonnaise or salad
    dressing
2 tablespoons finely chopped
    green onions
4 (½-inch-thick) slices
    sourdough bread, toasted

1 (6-oz.) pkg. thinly sliced
    oven-roasted chicken breast
1 pear, thinly sliced
1 oz. (¼ cup) shredded
    reduced-fat sharp Cheddar
    cheese
⅛ teaspoon paprika, if desired

Broiler Directions: 1. In small bowl, combine mayonnaise and green onions. Spread evenly on toasted bread slices. Layer chicken and pear slices evenly over bread. Place on broiler pan.
2. Broil 4 to 6 inches from heat for 5 minutes. Sprinkle evenly with cheese; broil an additional 1 to 2 minutes, or until cheese is melted. Sprinkle with paprika.

Yield: 4 sandwiches

Microwave Directions: 1. Prepare sandwiches as directed above; sprinkle with cheese. Place 1 sandwich on microwave-safe plate lined with microwave-safe paper towel.
2. Microwave on HIGH for 1 to 2 minutes, or until cheese is melted. Repeat with remaining sandwiches. Sprinkle with paprika.

Nutrition Information Per Serving
Serving Size: 1 Sandwich • Calories 250 • Calories from Fat 90 • Total Fat 10 g
Saturated Fat 3 g • Cholesterol 45 mg • Sodium 380 mg • Dietary Fiber 2 g
Dietary Exchanges: 1½ Starch, 2 Lean Meat, ½ Fat OR
1½ Carbohydrate, 2 Lean Meat, ½ Fat

About Pears

A firm-textured pear, such as Bosc, works best in this recipe.

About Sourdough Bread

Sourdough bread, a San Francisco specialty, gets its slightly tangy flavor from being leavened with a special fermented "starter dough" instead of ordinary yeast.

Chicken Pita Taquitos

30 min. or less   low-fat

About Pita Bread

Pita bread, a Middle Eastern staple, begins as a solid piece of dough that puffs up during baking, leaving a hollow pocket.

Ingredient Substitution

Wrap the chicken mixture in a tortilla instead of filling pita breads.

Recipe Variation

For a savory summer salad, cook the ingredients as directed and cool them. Toss with torn lettuce and your favorite vinaigrette. Serve with tortilla chips.

Prep Time: 20 minutes

2 (4-oz.) marinated mesquite barbecue-flavored chicken breast fillets or 1 (8.25-oz.) pkg. frozen mesquite-grilled chicken fillets
1 small zucchini, halved lengthwise, sliced crosswise
1 small onion, sliced
½ medium green bell pepper, thinly sliced

1 cup frozen whole kernel corn
1 large tomato, chopped
½ jalapeño chile pepper, seeded, finely chopped
1 tablespoon chopped fresh cilantro
3 (6-inch) whole wheat pita (pocket) breads, cut in half

1. Prepare chicken according to package directions until fork-tender and juices run clear.
2. Meanwhile, spray large nonstick skillet with nonstick cooking spray. Heat over medium-high heat until hot. Add zucchini, onion and bell pepper; cook and stir 4 minutes. Reduce heat to low. Stir in corn, tomato, chile pepper and cilantro; simmer 3 minutes, or until vegetables are tender and mixture is thoroughly heated, stirring occasionally.
3. Thinly slice cooked chicken; stir into vegetable mixture. Fill each pita bread half with about ⅔ cup chicken and vegetable mixture.

Yield: 6 sandwiches

Nutrition Information Per Serving
Serving Size: 2 Sandwiches • Calories 360 • Calories from Fat 50 • Total Fat 6 g
Saturated Fat 1 g • Cholesterol 35 mg • Sodium 750 mg • Dietary Fiber 8 g
Dietary Exchanges: 3 Starch, 2 Vegetable, 1 Lean Meat OR
3 Carbohydrate, 2 Vegetable, 1 Lean Meat

Chicken Pita Taquitos

Chicken Quesadillas

Prep Time: 20 minutes

2 cups cubed cooked chicken
4 oz. (1 cup) shredded taco-flavored Cheddar cheese
2 cups purchased thick and chunky salsa

2 tablespoons margarine or butter, softened
8 (8- to 10-inch) flour tortillas
½ cup sour cream

1. Heat griddle or large skillet to 375°F. In large bowl, combine chicken, cheese and 1 cup of the salsa. Spread margarine on 1 side of each tortilla.
2. Place 1 tortilla, margarine side down, on hot griddle. Top with ¾ cup chicken mixture. Place second tortilla, margarine side up, on chicken mixture. Cook until bottom is lightly browned. Turn quesadilla over; cook on second side until quesadilla is lightly browned and chicken mixture is thoroughly heated. Repeat with remaining tortillas and chicken mixture.
3. To serve, cut each quesadilla into 4 wedges; top with remaining 1 cup salsa and sour cream.

Yield: 4 quesadillas

Nutrition Information Per Serving

Serving Size: 1 Quesadilla • Calories 630 • Calories from Fat 280 • Total Fat 31 g
Saturated Fat 14 g • Cholesterol 105 mg • Sodium 860 mg • Dietary Fiber 4 g
Dietary Exchanges: 3 Starch, 1 Vegetable, 3½ Lean Meat, 4 Fat OR
3 Carbohydrate, 1 Vegetable, 3½ Lean Meat, 4 Fat

Recipe Fact

Queso is the Spanish word for cheese. A quesadilla is the Mexican equivalent of a grilled cheese sandwich—cheese melted between two tortillas.

Healthy Hint

To reduce the fat by 10 grams per serving and the calories by 100, coat the pan with nonstick cooking spray instead of buttering the tortillas and top the quesadillas with nonfat sour cream instead of regular sour cream.

Chicken Quesadillas

Grilled Chicken Vegetable Fajitas

Prep Time: 30 minutes

Kitchen Tip

If you choose avocado slices as a garnish, be sure to dip each piece in lemon or lime juice to prevent discoloration.

Recipe Variation

Omit the tortillas and serve the chicken and vegetables with white or brown rice.

¼ cup lime juice
1 tablespoon olive oil or vegetable oil
2 teaspoons chili powder
2 teaspoons minced garlic (2 to 4 cloves)
4 boneless, skinless chicken breast halves
2 medium red bell peppers, quartered

2 medium zucchini, cut in half lengthwise and crosswise
8 (8-inch) flour tortillas

Toppings, If Desired
Chopped tomatoes, avocado slices, chopped cilantro, sour cream and/or salsa

1. Heat grill. In small bowl, combine lime juice, oil, chili powder and garlic; mix well. Brush mixture over chicken breast halves, bell peppers and zucchini. Let stand at room temperature 10 minutes to marinate.

2. When ready to grill, place chicken, bell peppers and zucchini on gas grill over medium heat or on charcoal grill 4 to 6 inches from medium coals. Cook 8 to 10 minutes, or until vegetables are tender, and chicken is fork-tender and juices run clear, turning once.

3. To serve, slice chicken and vegetables; place in center of each tortilla. Top with desired toppings; roll up.

Yield: 8 fajitas

Tip: To broil, place chicken on broiler pan and broil 4 to 6 inches from heat using times provided above as a guide.

Nutrition Information Per Serving

Serving Size: 2 Fajitas • Calories 550 • Calories from Fat 200 • Total Fat 22 g
Saturated Fat 5 g • Cholesterol 80 mg • Sodium 550 mg • Dietary Fiber 8 g
Dietary Exchanges: 3 Starch, 2 Vegetable, 3 Lean Meat, 2½ Fat OR
3 Carbohydrate, 2 Vegetable, 3 Lean Meat, 2½ Fat

Hearty Chicken and Cheese Calzones

30 min. or less

Prep Time: 30 minutes

2 oz. (½ cup) shredded Cheddar cheese

2 oz. (½ cup) shredded Swiss cheese

1 cup chopped cooked chicken

½ cup chopped green or red bell pepper

¼ teaspoon dried basil leaves

1 (10-oz.) can refrigerated pizza crust

1. Heat oven to 425°F. Grease cookie sheet. In medium bowl, combine all ingredients except pizza crust; mix well. Press pizza crust into 14 × 8-inch rectangle on greased cookie sheet. Cut into four 7 × 4-inch rectangles; separate slightly.

2. Spoon about ½ cup chicken and cheese mixture onto one half of each rectangle; fold crust over filling. Press edges with fork to seal; prick tops with fork. Repeat with remaining pizza crust rectangles and chicken and cheese mixture.

3. Bake at 425°F. for 11 to 16 minutes, or until golden brown.

Yield: 4 calzones

Kitchen Tip

To give the calzones a shiny top, brush them with a slightly beaten egg white before baking.

Healthy Hint

Reduce the fat to 8 grams per calzone by substituting reduced-fat cheeses for the regular.

Nutrition Information Per Serving

Serving Size: 1 Calzone • Calories 350 • Calories from Fat 120 • Total Fat 13 g
Saturated Fat 7 g • Cholesterol 60 mg • Sodium 500 mg • Dietary Fiber 1 g
Dietary Exchanges: 2 Starch, 2½ Medium-Fat Meat OR
2 Carbohydrate, 2½ Medium-Fat Meat

Hot Chicken Hoagie

Prep Time: 15 minutes

About Tomatoes

Like many fruits, tomatoes will continue to ripen after they've been picked. Pick any green tomatoes left on the vine when a hard frost threatens in the fall and ripen them indoors on the windowsill.

Healthy Hint

To reduce the fat in each hoagie by 13 grams, cut the bacon to two slices and crumble it to disperse the flavor, use low-fat ranch dressing instead of regular and substitute alfalfa sprouts for the avocado.

Make It Special

Add shredded fresh basil just before serving.

1 (10- or 10.5-oz.) pkg. frozen breaded chicken breast patties
1 (1-lb.) loaf French bread, cut in half lengthwise*
½ cup purchased ranch salad dressing

6 leaves lettuce
8 slices bacon, cooked until crisp
1 medium avocado, thinly sliced
1 medium tomato, thinly sliced

1. Prepare chicken breast patties as directed on package.
2. Meanwhile, spread cut sides of bread halves with salad dressing. Layer bottom half of bread with lettuce, bacon, chicken patties, avocado and tomato. Cover with top half of bread. If desired, secure sandwich with skewers or picks. To serve, cut into slices.

Yield: 6 servings

***Tip:** If desired, 6 split kaiser rolls can be substituted for the French bread.

Nutrition Information Per Serving

Serving Size: ⅙ of Recipe • Calories 580 • Calories from Fat 300 • Total Fat 33 g
Saturated Fat 8 g • Cholesterol 40 mg • Sodium 1060 mg • Dietary Fiber 5 g
Dietary Exchanges: 3½ Starch, 1 Lean Meat, 6 Fat OR
3½ Carbohydrate, 1 Lean Meat, 6 Fat

Hot Chicken Hoagie

Monterey Chicken Fillet Sandwiches

30 min. or less • editor's choice

About Monterey Jack Cheese

Monterey Jack, a mild, soft-textured cheese, originated in Monterey, California, and is sometimes called California Jack or simply Jack cheese. A hard version can be grated as an alternative to Parmesan.

Prep Time: 25 minutes

4 boneless, skinless chicken breast halves
½ cup plain bread crumbs
½ teaspoon garlic salt
¼ cup all-purpose flour
1 egg, beaten
3 tablespoons oil
4 (5½- to 6-inch) French rolls,

ranch rolls or hoagie buns, halved lengthwise
8 teaspoons mayonnaise or salad dressing
1 cup shredded lettuce
4 medium tomato slices
4 (1-oz.) slices Monterey Jack cheese

1. Place 1 chicken breast half between 2 pieces of plastic wrap or waxed paper. Working from center, gently pound chicken with flat side of meat mallet or rolling pin until about ¼ inch thick; remove wrap. Repeat with remaining chicken breast halves.
2. In small, shallow bowl, combine bread crumbs and garlic salt. Coat both sides of chicken breast halves with flour. Dip each in egg; coat both sides with crumb mixture.
3. Heat oil in large skillet over medium-high heat until hot. Add chicken; cook 6 to 8 minutes on each side, or until lightly browned and juices run clear.
4. Meanwhile, place French rolls, cut side up, on ungreased cookie sheet. Broil 4 to 6 inches from heat for 1 to 2 minutes, or until toasted; remove top halves of rolls from cookie sheet. Spread bottom halves of rolls with mayonnaise; top with lettuce, tomato, chicken and cheese. Broil 4 to 6 inches from heat for 1 minute, or until cheese is melted; cover with top halves of rolls.

Yield: 4 sandwiches

Nutrition Information Per Serving

Serving Size: 1 Sandwich • Calories 780 • Calories from Fat 320 • Total Fat 36 g
Saturated Fat 10 g • Cholesterol 155 mg • Sodium 1240 mg • Dietary Fiber 3 g
Dietary Exchanges: 4 Starch, 1 Vegetable, 4 Medium-Fat Meat, 3 Fat OR
4 Carbohydrate, 1 Vegetable, 4 Medium-Fat Meat, 3 Fat

Peppered Grilled Chicken Sandwiches

Prep Time: 20 minutes

4 boneless, skinless chicken breast halves

2 to 3 teaspoons sweet hot mustard

1 to 2 teaspoons coarsely ground black pepper

4 large whole wheat sandwich buns, split, toasted if desired

8 teaspoons purchased thousand island salad dressing

4 leaves lettuce

4 medium tomato slices

1. Heat grill. Place 1 chicken breast half between 2 pieces of plastic wrap or waxed paper. Working from center, gently pound chicken with flat side of meat mallet or rolling pin until about ¼ inch thick; remove wrap. Repeat with remaining chicken breast halves. Spread chicken with mustard; sprinkle with pepper.

2. When ready to grill, place chicken on gas grill over medium heat or on charcoal grill 4 to 6 inches from medium-high coals. Cook 8 to 10 minutes, or until chicken is fork-tender and juices run clear, turning once.

3. Spread cut sides of buns with dressing. Layer lettuce, tomato and chicken on bottom half of buns; cover with top half of buns.

Yield: 4 sandwiches

Tip: To broil, place chicken on broiler pan and broil 4 to 6 inches from heat using times provided above as a guide.

Nutrition Information Per Serving

Serving Size: 1 Sandwich • Calories 310 • Calories from Fat 80 • Total Fat 9 g
Saturated Fat 2 g • Cholesterol 75 mg • Sodium 390 mg • Dietary Fiber 4 g
Dietary Exchanges: 1½ Starch, 4 Very Lean Meat, 1 Fat OR
1½ Carbohydrate, 4 Very Lean Meat, 1 Fat

Make It Special

Add strips of roasted red, yellow and green pepper to the sandwich.

Menu Suggestion

Serve the sandwich with a relish tray of cucumber spears, carrot and celery sticks, one or two kinds of olives and pickled peppers.

No-Bake Salad Pizza

Prep Time: 15 minutes

Healthy Hint

Compare the labels of purchased bread shells or pizza crusts if you're watching fat and calories; ingredients and nutrition can vary widely.

Make It Special

Mince the toppings extra fine and cut the pizza into little squares for a great party appetizer.

No-Bake Salad Pizza

1 cup purchased spinach dip
1 (10-oz.) thin-crust Italian
   bread shell
1 cup chopped broccoli

1 cup cubed cooked chicken
⅓ cup sliced green onions
1 small tomato, seeded,
   chopped

Spread spinach dip evenly over bread shell to within ½ inch of edge. Top with remaining ingredients. Cut into 8 wedges to serve.

Yield: 8 servings

Nutrition Information Per Serving
Serving Size: ⅛ of Recipe • Calories 230 • Calories from Fat 110 • Total Fat 12 g
Saturated Fat 4 g • Cholesterol 30 mg • Sodium 330 mg • Dietary Fiber 1 g
Dietary Exchanges: 1 Starch, 1 Vegetable, 1 Lean Meat, 1½ Fat OR
1 Carbohydrate, 1 Vegetable, 1 Lean Meat, 1½ Fat

Rosemary Chicken and Brie en Croûte

Prep Time: 20 minutes
(Ready in 50 minutes)

1 (8-oz.) can refrigerated
  crescent dinner rolls
2 tablespoons finely chopped
  green onions
6 oz. Brie cheese, rind
  removed, cubed
1½ cups chopped cooked
  chicken breast

1 egg, beaten
1 teaspoon dried rosemary
  leaves, crushed
1 tablespoon grated Parmesan
  cheese
8 medium tomato wedges
4 green onions

1. Heat oven to 350°F. Separate dough into 4 rectangles; firmly press perforations to seal. Spoon ¼ of green onions onto center of each rectangle; top with ¼ of cheese cubes. Top each with ¼ of chicken, pressing into cheese. Fold short ends of dough rectangles over chicken, overlapping slightly. Fold open ends over about ½ inch to form rectangle. Pinch edges to seal. Place, seam side down, on ungreased 15 × 10 × 1-inch baking pan or cookie sheet. Cut three 1-inch slashes on top of each roll. Brush with egg; sprinkle with rosemary and Parmesan cheese.

2. Bake at 350°F. for 21 to 26 minutes, or until golden brown. Let stand 5 minutes before serving. Garnish each sandwich with 2 tomato wedges and 1 green onion.

Yield: 4 sandwiches

Nutrition Information Per Serving

Serving Size: 1 Sandwich • Calories 460 • Calories from Fat 240 • Total Fat 27 g
Saturated Fat 11 g • Cholesterol 140 mg • Sodium 760 mg • Dietary Fiber 1 g
Dietary Exchanges: 1½ Starch, 3½ Medium-Fat Meat, 2 Fat OR
1½ Carbohydrate, 3½ Medium-Fat Meat, 2 Fat

Recipe Fact

En croûte is the French term for "in a crust."

About Brie

Brie, a creamy-soft, rich and distinctively flavored French cheese, comes encased in a slightly rubbery white crust. The crust is edible (though some people find it too strong-flavored), but it's usually cut away for recipes in which the cheese is cooked. When melted, Brie develops a satiny, runny consistency.

Kitchen Tip

For easier cleanup, line the baking pan with aluminum foil.

Spicy Chinese Chicken Tacos

● 30 min. or less ● low-fat

Recipe Variation

Toss the chicken mixture with cooked Chinese noodles or thin spaghetti instead of filling the taco shell.

Make It Special

Garnish each plate with orange slices atop a curly lettuce leaf.

Menu Suggestion

Serve with a scoop of rice and a tossed salad made with lettuce, radishes, celery and a light sweet-and-sour dressing.

Prep Time: 25 minutes

3 boneless, skinless chicken breast halves, cut into thin strips
1 teaspoon grated gingerroot
1 small garlic clove, minced
2 tablespoons soy sauce
1 tablespoon honey
1 large green onion, sliced
½ teaspoon crushed red pepper flakes
1 (4.6-oz.) pkg. (12) taco shells, heated
1½ cups shredded lettuce

1. Spray large nonstick skillet with nonstick cooking spray. Heat over medium-high heat until hot. Add chicken, gingerroot and garlic; cook and stir 3 to 5 minutes, or until lightly browned. Reduce heat to low.
2. Add soy sauce, honey, green onion and crushed red pepper flakes; stir to coat. Cover; cook over low heat for 5 minutes, or until chicken is no longer pink, stirring occasionally.
3. To serve, place scant ¼ cup chicken in each taco shell. Top each with lettuce.

Yield: 12 tacos

Nutrition Information Per Serving
Serving Size: 2 Tacos • Calories 200 • Calories from Fat 70 • Total Fat 8 g
Saturated Fat 1 g • Cholesterol 35 mg • Sodium 460 mg • Dietary Fiber 2 g
Dietary Exchanges: 1 Starch, 2 Very Lean Meat, 1 Fat OR
1 Carbohydrate, 2 Very Lean Meat, 1 Fat

Spicy Chinese Chicken Tacos

Tarragon Chicken Burgers

Prep Time: 30 minutes

Make It Special

Give these burgers a French flair by topping them with a slice of Brie, slices of tomato and leaf lettuce.

Menu Suggestion

Serve chicken burgers alongside potato salad spiked with fresh dill, buttered corn on the cob and tender raw baby carrots. End the meal with sorbet topped with fresh berries.

1 lb. ground chicken
1 tablespoon chopped fresh tarragon or 1 teaspoon dried tarragon leaves
1 tablespoon finely chopped onion
1 tablespoon sour cream
⅛ teaspoon salt
4 burger buns, split

Grill Directions: 1. Heat grill. In large bowl, combine all ingredients except buns; mix gently. (Mixture will be moist.) Shape mixture into 4 patties.

2. When ready to grill, oil grill rack. Place patties on gas grill over medium-low heat or on charcoal grill 4 to 6 inches from medium coals. Cook 9 to 13 minutes, or until no longer pink in center, turning once. Serve in burger buns.

Yield: 4 burgers

Broiler Directions: 1. Prepare patties as directed above. Oil broiler pan. Place patties on oiled pan.

2. Broil 4 to 6 inches from heat for 9 to 13 minutes, or until center is no longer pink, turning once. Serve in burger buns.

Nutrition Information Per Serving

Serving Size: 1 Burger • Calories 310 • Calories from Fat 120 • Total Fat 13 g
Saturated 4 g • Cholesterol 90 mg • Sodium 390 mg • Dietary Fiber 1 g
Dietary Exchanges: 1½ Starch, 2½ Medium-Fat Meat OR
1½ Carbohydrate, 2½ Medium-Fat Meat

Chicken and Black Bean Burritos

30 min. or less • low-fat • editor's choice

Prep time: 30 minutes

1 tablespoon oil
3 boneless, skinless chicken breast halves, cut into thin strips
1 (15-oz.) can black beans, drained, rinsed
3 tablespoons water
½ teaspoon cumin
1 garlic clove, minced

2 to 3 drops hot pepper sauce
6 (8- to 10-inch) flour tortillas
6 leaves lettuce
1 small tomato, seeded, chopped
¼ cup sliced green onions
2 tablespoons chopped fresh cilantro

1. Heat oven to 350°F. Heat oil in large skillet over medium-high heat until hot. Add chicken; cook and stir 5 minutes, or until chicken is no longer pink. Remove from skillet; cover to keep warm.

2. In same skillet, combine beans, water, cumin, garlic and hot pepper sauce; mix well. Cook over medium-high heat until thoroughly heated, stirring occasionally and mashing beans slightly.

3. Meanwhile, wrap tortillas in foil. Bake at 350°F. for 10 minutes, or until warm.

4. Place 1 lettuce leaf on each warm tortilla; spoon about 2 tablespoons bean mixture down center of each. Top each with ⅓ cup cooked chicken; sprinkle with tomato, green onions and cilantro. Fold sides of each tortilla over filling, overlapping to form triangle.

Yield: 6 burritos

Nutrition Information Per Serving

Serving Size: 1 Burrito • Calories 340 • Calories from Fat 70 • Total Fat 8 g
Saturated Fat 1 g • Cholesterol 35 mg • Sodium 310 mg • Dietary Fiber 6 g
Dietary Exchanges: 3 Starch, 2 Lean Meat OR 3 Carbohydrate, 2 Lean Meat

Recipe Fact

A burrito is a Mexican "sandwich" consisting of a mixture of meat and/or vegetables wrapped in a flour tortilla.

About Flour Tortillas

Flour tortillas predominate in northern Mexico; corn tortillas are preferred in central and southern Mexico. While corn tortillas are nearly fat-free (about a gram of fat), traditional recipes for the flour variety usually include a little lard, although low- and nonfat flour tortillas are now available.

Kitchen Tip

To make slicing the raw chicken easier, firm it in the freezer for half an hour or so before cutting.

ws and Chilies

Fond memories of home might well include a steaming bowl of chicken soup on a frosty day. If you're an avid soup fan, you'll be pleased to find some innovative recipes for chill-chasing chilies and stews as well as traditional soups. And, if you're new to making stockpot concoctions from scratch, you'll be delighted to find how easy it is.

Soups, Stews and Chilies

Previous page: Chicken and Pasta Chowder page 99

Chicken and Pasta Chowder

Prep Time: 35 minutes

3 boneless, skinless chicken
   breast halves, cut into bite-
   sized pieces
1 medium onion, chopped
2 garlic cloves, minced
2 (14½-oz.) cans ready-to-
   serve chicken or vegetable
   broth
1 teaspoon dried basil leaves
½ teaspoon salt

2½ oz. (¾ cup) uncooked
   rotini (spiral pasta)
1 (1-lb.) pkg. frozen broccoli,
   carrots and cauliflower
4 cups skim milk
½ cup all-purpose flour
½ medium red bell pepper,
   chopped
1 oz. (¼ cup) shredded fresh
   Parmesan cheese

1. Spray nonstick Dutch oven or large saucepan with nonstick cooking spray. Heat over medium heat until hot. Add chicken, onion and garlic; cook 4 to 6 minutes, or until onion is tender, stirring occasionally.
2. Stir in broth, basil and salt. Bring to a boil. Add rotini; cook over medium-high heat for 8 minutes, stirring occasionally.
3. Meanwhile, place frozen vegetables in colander or strainer; rinse with warm water until thawed. Drain well. In small bowl, combine 1 cup of the milk and flour; blend well.
4. Stir vegetables, milk mixture, remaining 3 cups milk and bell pepper into rotini mixture. Bring just to a boil, stirring frequently. Reduce heat to medium; cook 3 to 5 minutes, or until soup thickens and vegetables and pasta are tender, stirring occasionally.
5. Ladle chowder into bowls; top with cheese.

Yield: 6 (1⅔-cup) servings

Nutrition Information Per Serving

Serving Size: 1⅔ Cups • Calories 270 • Calories from Fat 35 • Total Fat 4 g
Saturated Fat 1 g • Cholesterol 40 mg • Sodium 810 mg • Dietary Fiber 3 g
Dietary Exchanges: 2 Starch, 1 Vegetable, 1½ Lean Meat OR
2 Carbohydrate, 1 Vegetable, 1½ Lean Meat

About Parmesan Cheese

When a recipe calls for Parmesan cheese, treat yourself to fresh-grated. Buy your own small block of Parmesan to grate, or purchase grated Parmesan, sold in bags alongside other grated cheeses. The fresh-grated has more pungent flavor than the familiar granular variety sold in cans.

Ingredient Substitution

If you don't have rotini on hand, use another pasta shape such as bow-tie pasta, wagon wheel pasta, radiatore, shell pasta or macaroni. Pimiento from a jar can be used instead of the red bell pepper, and any vegetables can be used in place of the broccoli, carrot and cauliflower mixture.

Brunswick Stew

Prep Time: 40 minutes

2 tablespoons margarine or butter
½ cup chopped onion
1 medium green bell pepper, chopped
2 cups chicken broth
2 cups cubed cooked chicken
1 (14.5- or 16-oz.) can whole tomatoes, undrained, cut up
1 (15.5-oz.) can butter beans, drained

1 (7-oz.) can vacuum-packed whole kernel corn, undrained
¼ teaspoon salt
⅛ teaspoon pepper
⅛ to ¼ teaspoon crushed red pepper flakes
½ cup sliced fresh or frozen okra
3 tablespoons all-purpose flour
⅓ cup water

1. In large saucepan, melt margarine over medium-high heat. Add onion and bell pepper; cook and stir until crisp-tender. Stir in chicken broth, chicken, tomatoes, beans, corn, salt, pepper and crushed red pepper flakes. Bring to a boil. Reduce heat to low; simmer 15 minutes. Add okra; simmer an additional 5 minutes, or until okra is tender.
2. In small bowl, combine flour and water; blend until smooth. Stir into chicken mixture. Cook over medium heat until mixture boils and thickens, stirring constantly.

Yield: 6 servings

Nutrition Information Per Serving

Serving Size: ⅙ of Recipe • Calories 230 • Calories from Fat 70 • Total Fat 8 g
Saturated Fat 2 g • Cholesterol 40 mg • Sodium 780 mg • Dietary Fiber 4 g
Dietary Exchanges: 1 Starch, 1 Vegetable, 2 Lean Meat OR
1 Carbohydrate, 1 Vegetable, 2 Lean Meat

Cassoulet

Prep Time: 20 minutes
(Ready in 15 hours 20 minutes)

1 (16-oz.) pkg. dried navy
   beans
4 cups water
4 boneless, skinless chicken
   breast halves, cut into
   1-inch pieces
8 oz. cooked ham, cut into
   1-inch pieces
3 large carrots, sliced
2 medium onions, coarsely
   chopped

1 rib celery, sliced
$\frac{1}{4}$ cup firmly packed brown
   sugar
$\frac{1}{2}$ teaspoon salt
$\frac{1}{4}$ teaspoon dry mustard
$\frac{1}{4}$ teaspoon pepper
1 (8-oz.) can tomato sauce
2 tablespoons molasses

1. Sort beans. Rinse well; drain. In 3½- or 4-quart slow cooker, combine beans and water. Soak at least 8 hours or overnight.

2. Cover; cook on high setting for 3 hours.

3. Add remaining ingredients; mix well. Cover; cook on high setting for an additional 3 to 4 hours, or until beans are tender and chicken is no longer pink.

Yield: 10 (1-cup) servings

Nutrition Information Per Serving

Serving Size: 1 Cup • Calories 300 • Calories from Fat 25 • Total Fat 3 g
Saturated Fat 1 g • Cholesterol 40 mg • Sodium 610 mg • Dietary Fiber 11 g
Dietary Exchanges: 3 Starch, 2 Very Lean Meat OR
3 Carbohydrate, 2 Very Lean Meat

About Navy Beans

Navy beans, actually white in color, get their name from their role as a menu staple of the U.S. Navy since the 1880s. Sometimes called Yankee beans, they are a good source of fiber. Before cooking, sort through the beans to remove any debris and rinse well.

Kitchen Tip

If you don't have a slow cooker, soak the beans overnight in 6 to 8 cups of water and drain them. Then proceed with the recipe as directed, simmering the ingredients in a stockpot or Dutch oven. For same-day cooking, sort and rinse the beans, then cover with 6 to 8 cups of water and bring them to a hard boil for about 3 minutes. Remove the pot from the heat, cover and let the beans stand for about an hour, then drain and continue with the recipe.

Chicken and Cabbage Panade

Recipe Fact

Panade (puh-NAHD) is the French name for a soup that contains bread.

Recipe Variation

Add a 15-ounce can of crushed tomatoes and 1 tablespoon of caraway seed or dill seed.

Prep Time: 20 minutes
(Ready in 1 hour 5 minutes)

¼ cup margarine or butter
4 cups coarsely shredded cabbage
1 cup thinly sliced carrots
1 cup chopped onions
2 boneless, skinless chicken breast halves, cut into thin strips

12 (½-inch-thick) slices French bread, toasted
3 tablespoons grated Parmesan cheese
2 (14½-oz.) cans ready-to-serve chicken broth
4 oz. (1 cup) shredded Swiss cheese

1. Heat oven to 350°F. In large skillet, melt margarine over medium-high heat. Add cabbage, carrots, onions and chicken; cook until chicken is no longer pink and vegetables are tender, stirring occasionally.

2. Place 4 slices of bread in bottom of ungreased 2½- to 3-quart casserole. Spoon half of cabbage mixture over bread; sprinkle with 1 tablespoon of the Parmesan cheese. Repeat with 4 slices of bread, remaining cabbage mixture and 1 tablespoon of the Parmesan cheese. Top with remaining bread. Pour chicken broth over bread and cabbage mixture.

3. Bake at 350°F. for 20 minutes. Sprinkle with Swiss cheese and remaining 1 tablespoon Parmesan cheese. Bake an additional 20 to 25 minutes, or until edges are bubbly. Serve in soup plates or bowls.

Yield: 6 servings

Nutrition Information Per Serving

Serving Size: ⅙ of Recipe • Calories 350 • Calories from Fat 150 • Total Fat 17 g
Saturated Fat 6 g • Cholesterol 45 mg • Sodium 880 mg • Dietary Fiber 3 g
Dietary Exchanges: 1 Starch, 2 Vegetable, 2 Lean Meat 2 Fat OR
1 Carbohydrate, 2 Vegetable, 2 Lean Meat, 2 Fat

Chicken and Cabbage Panade

Chicken and Sweet Potato Stew

Prep Time: 50 minutes

About Sweet Potatoes

Orange-fleshed sweet potatoes are often mistakenly sold as "yams." Although the two terms are often used interchangeably, a yam is actually a different vegetable. True yams are native to Africa and a common Caribbean ingredient, but these are very rare in U.S. markets—despite what the sign in the supermarket says.

Kitchen Tip

Cube the sweet potatoes immediately before adding to the pot to prevent them from discoloring.

Make-Ahead Tip

Cook and refrigerate the stew up to two days before serving. Reheat over low heat.

$\frac{1}{4}$ cup all-purpose flour
$\frac{1}{4}$ teaspoon garlic salt
3 boneless, skinless chicken breast halves, cut into 1-inch pieces
1 tablespoon oil
1 medium onion, quartered, sliced

$1\frac{1}{2}$ cups apple juice or cider
2 cups cubed ($\frac{1}{2}$-inch) peeled sweet potatoes
2 (14.5-oz.) cans no-salt-added tomatoes, drained, cut up
1 teaspoon dried basil leaves

1. In large plastic bag, combine flour and garlic salt. Add chicken; shake until coated.

2. Heat oil in nonstick Dutch oven or large saucepan over medium-high heat until hot. Add chicken; cook 3 minutes, or just until browned. Remove chicken from Dutch oven.

3. Add onion to Dutch oven; cook and stir 2 minutes, or until tender, adding some apple juice if necessary to prevent sticking. Stir in remaining apple juice, sweet potatoes, tomatoes, basil and chicken. Bring to a boil. Reduce heat to low; simmer 30 to 35 minutes, or until chicken is no longer pink and potatoes are tender, stirring occasionally.

Yield: 4 (1$\frac{3}{4}$-cup) servings

Nutrition Information Per Serving

Serving Size: 1¾ Cups • Calories 330 • Calories from Fat 50 • Total Fat 6 g
Saturated Fat 1 g • Cholesterol 55 mg • Sodium 200 mg • Dietary Fiber 5 g
Dietary Exchanges: 2 Starch, 2 Lean Meat OR 2 Carbohydrate, 2 Lean Meat

Chicken Wild Rice Soup

Prep Time: 15 minutes
(Ready in 1 hour)

2 cups water

3 (10½-oz.) cans condensed
chicken broth

½ cup uncooked wild rice*

½ cup finely chopped green
onions

½ cup margarine or butter

¾ cup all-purpose flour

½ teaspoon salt

¼ teaspoon poultry seasoning

⅛ teaspoon pepper

2 cups half-and-half

1½ cups cubed cooked chicken

8 slices bacon, cooked until
crisp, crumbled

1 tablespoon diced pimiento

2 to 3 tablespoons dry sherry,
if desired

About Wild Rice

Wild rice is actually a grass that grows in marshy areas. Native to Minnesota and Wisconsin, most wild rice is no longer "wild" and much of it is now grown in California. The nutty grain lends smoky flavor to this rich, creamy soup.

1. In Dutch oven or large saucepan, combine water and broth. Add wild rice and green onions. Bring to a boil. Reduce heat to low; cover and simmer 45 to 55 minutes, or until rice is tender.

2. In medium saucepan, melt margarine over medium heat. Stir in flour, salt, poultry seasoning and pepper. Cook 1 minute, or until smooth and bubbly, stirring constantly. Gradually stir in half-and-half; cook until slightly thickened, stirring constantly. Slowly add half-and-half mixture to rice mixture, stirring constantly. Add remaining ingredients. Cook over low heat until thoroughly heated, stirring frequently. DO NOT BOIL.

Yield: 6 (1½-cup) servings

*Tip: Uncooked regular long-grain white rice can be substituted for the wild rice; reduce simmering time to 20 to 30 minutes, or until rice is tender.

Nutrition Information Per Serving

Serving Size: 1½ Cups • Calories 520 • Calories from Fat 300 • Total Fat 33 g
Saturated Fat 11 g • Cholesterol 70 mg • Sodium 1490 mg • Dietary Fiber 2 g
Dietary Exchanges: 2 Starch, 3 Lean Meat, 4½ Fat OR
2 Carbohydrate, 3 Lean Meat, 4½ Fat

Chicken Cider Stew

Kitchen Tip

To avoid lumps in the thickening mixture, add the cider to the flour a little at a time, not the other way around.

Recipe Variation

Instead of using the flour and cider mixture to thicken the stew, simmer 2 large apples, peeled and diced, along with the other ingredients.

Menu Suggestion

Ladle each serving of the stew onto plates of broad egg noodles and pass a basket of warmed rolls.

Prep Time: 20 minutes
(Ready in 1 hour 5 minutes)

4 slices bacon, cut into ½-inch pieces
½ teaspoon dried basil leaves
⅛ teaspoon pepper
3 to 3½ lb. cut-up frying chicken, skin removed, if desired

3½ cups apple cider or juice
¼ cup ketchup
1 cup thinly sliced carrots
1 medium onion, quartered
1 (8-oz.) pkg. frozen cut green beans in a pouch
¼ cup all-purpose flour

1. In Dutch oven or large saucepan, cook bacon over medium-high heat until crisp. Remove bacon from Dutch oven. Reserve drippings in Dutch oven. In small bowl, combine basil and pepper; mix well. Rub onto chicken pieces. Brown chicken in hot bacon drippings, turning to brown all sides; drain. Remove chicken from Dutch oven.

2. Add 3 cups of the apple cider and the ketchup to Dutch oven; blend well. Add chicken, carrots, onion and green beans. Bring to a boil. Reduce heat to low; cover and simmer 45 minutes, or until chicken is fork-tender and juices run clear.

3. In small bowl, combine flour and remaining ½ cup apple cider; blend well. Gradually stir into hot chicken mixture. Cook and stir until stew is thickened and bubbly. Stir in bacon. If desired, add salt and pepper to taste.

Yield: 6 (1⅓-cup) servings

Nutrition Information Per Serving

Serving Size: 1⅓ Cups • Calories 310 • Calories from Fat 80 • Total Fat 9 g
Saturated Fat 3 g • Cholesterol 80 mg • Sodium 330 mg • Dietary Fiber 2 g
Dietary Exchanges: 1 Starch, ½ Fruit, 1 Vegetable, 3 Lean Meat OR
1½ Carbohydrate, 1 Vegetable, 3 Lean Meat

Chicken Escarole Soup

Prep Time: 20 minutes

- **2 boneless, skinless chicken breast halves, cut into short strips**
- **¼ cup sliced green onions**
- **2 (14½-oz.) cans ready-to-serve fat-free chicken broth with ⅓ less sodium**
- **1 (14.5-oz.) can no-salt-added whole tomatoes, undrained, cut up**
- **½ teaspoon dried marjoram leaves**
- **⅛ teaspoon pepper**
- **2 cups shredded escarole or spinach**

Stovetop Directions: 1. Spray large nonstick saucepan with nonstick cooking spray. Heat over medium-high heat until hot. Add chicken and green onions; cook and stir until chicken is no longer pink.
2. Stir in remaining ingredients. Bring to a boil. Reduce heat to low; simmer 5 minutes, or until thoroughly heated.

Yield: 4 (1½-cup) servings

Microwave Directions: 1. In 2-quart microwave-safe casserole or bowl, combine chicken and green onions; cover tightly. Microwave on HIGH for 3½ to 4½ minutes, or until chicken is no longer pink, stirring once halfway through cooking.
2. Stir in chicken broth, tomatoes, marjoram and pepper; cover tightly. Microwave on HIGH for 7 to 8 minutes, or until very hot. Stir in escarole. Microwave on HIGH for 1 to 2 minutes.

Nutrition Information Per Serving

Serving Size: 1½ Cups • Calories 110 • Calories from Fat 20 • Total Fat 2 g
Saturated Fat 0 g • Cholesterol 35 mg • Sodium 530 mg • Dietary Fiber 2 g
Dietary Exchanges: 1½ Vegetable, 2 Very Lean Meat

About Escarole

Escarole's firm-textured green leaves hold up well during cooking. Uncooked, they make a hearty contribution in salads, too.

Make-Ahead Tip

Prepare the soup, except the escarole, and freeze in a 2-quart container. Be sure to leave an inch or so of headroom at the top of the container to allow for expansion. Reheat the soup in the microwave or on the stovetop and add the escarole just before serving.

Chicken Meatball and Noodle Soup

About Parsnips

Parsnips look like albino carrots and add a similar sweet flavor to soups and stews. They're also good cooked and mashed with turnips or potatoes. Sometimes they're dipped in wax to extend their shelf life. Remove the wax with a vegetable peeler.

Recipe Variation

Omit the soup and serve the mini meatballs with tomato sauce and pasta.

Prep Time: 45 minutes

Meatballs
1 egg, beaten
½ cup plain bread crumbs
½ teaspoon salt
¼ to ½ teaspoon pepper
1 lb. ground chicken breast

Soup
1 tablespoon oil
1 cup chopped onions
1 garlic clove, minced
4 cups water

3 (10½-oz.) cans condensed chicken broth
1 cup sliced carrots
1 cup sliced celery
1 cup sliced parsnips
½ teaspoon salt
¼ teaspoon pepper
1 bay leaf
3 oz. (1½ cups) uncooked medium egg noodles
¼ cup chopped fresh parsley

1. Heat oven to 400°F. Lightly grease 15 × 10 × 1-inch baking pan. In large bowl, combine all meatball ingredients; mix well. Using wet hands, shape into 1-inch balls.
2. Place meatballs on greased pan. Bake at 400°F. for 15 minutes, or until no longer pink in center, turning meatballs once during baking. Place on paper towels to drain.
3. Meanwhile, heat oil in Dutch oven or large saucepan over medium heat. Add onions and garlic; cook and stir 3 minutes. Add water, broth, carrots, celery, parsnips, ½ teaspoon salt, ¼ teaspoon pepper and bay leaf. Bring to a boil. Reduce heat to low; cover and simmer 5 minutes.
4. Stir in meatballs, noodles and parsley. Cook 8 to 12 minutes, or until vegetables and noodles are tender. Remove bay leaf.

Yield: 8 (1¼-cup) servings

Nutrition Information Per Serving
Serving Size: 1¼ Cups • Calories 220 • Calories from Fat 50 • Total Fat 6 g
Saturated Fat 1 g • Cholesterol 70 mg • Sodium 1080 mg • Dietary Fiber 2 g
Dietary Exchanges: 1 Starch, 1 Vegetable, 2 Lean Meat OR
1 Carbohydrate, 1 Vegetable, 2 Lean Meat

Chicken Meatball and Noodle Soup

Chicken 'n Dumplings with Vegetables

low-fat

Kitchen Tip

For the lightest, fluffiest dumplings, avoid the temptation to open the lid and peek before 25 minutes is up.

Prep Time: 25 minutes
(Ready in 55 minutes)

2 tablespoons margarine or butter
4 boneless, skinless chicken breast halves, cut into 1-inch pieces
1½ cups chopped onions
1 cup chopped celery
3 garlic cloves, minced
1 (1-lb.) pkg. frozen mixed vegetables

1 (14½-oz.) can ready-to-serve chicken broth
3 tablespoons chopped fresh parsley or 3 teaspoons dried parsley flakes
1½ teaspoons poultry seasoning
1 cup skim milk
½ cup all-purpose flour
1 (7.5-oz.) can refrigerated buttermilk biscuits

1. Melt margarine in Dutch oven or large saucepan over medium-high heat. Add chicken, onions, celery and garlic; cook 12 to 15 minutes, or until chicken is no longer pink, stirring occasionally.

2. Add mixed vegetables, broth, parsley and poultry seasoning; mix well. Bring to a boil, stirring frequently. In small bowl, combine milk and flour; blend until smooth. Add to chicken mixture; cook and stir until thickened and bubbly. Reduce heat to low.

3. Separate dough into 10 biscuits; cut each biscuit in half. Starting in center of Dutch oven, arrange biscuit halves on top of chicken mixture in spiral formation. Cover tightly; cook 25 to 30 minutes, or until biscuits are fluffy and no longer doughy.

Yield: 6 servings

Nutrition Information Per Serving
Serving Size: ⅙ of Recipe • Calories 340 • Calories from Fat 70 • Total Fat 8 g
Saturated Fat 2 g • Cholesterol 50 mg • Sodium 650 mg • Dietary Fiber 4 g
Dietary Exchanges: 2 Starch, 2 Vegetable, 2 Lean Meat, ½ Fat OR
2 Carbohydrate, 2 Vegetable, 2 Lean Meat, ½ Fat

Chicken, Red Beans and Rice Chili

Prep Time: 55 minutes

1 tablespoon oil
1½ lb. boneless, skinless
   chicken thighs, cut into
   ½-inch pieces
1 medium onion, chopped
½ cup uncooked regular long-
   grain white rice
2 (14.5-oz.) cans stewed
   tomatoes
1 (14½-oz.) can ready-to-serve
   chicken broth with ⅓ less
   sodium or 1¾ cups chicken
   broth

1¼ cups water
1 (15.5-oz.) can red beans,
   rinsed, drained
1 to 2 tablespoons chili powder
⅛ teaspoon salt
⅛ teaspoon pepper
4 to 8 drops hot pepper sauce,
   if desired

1. Heat oil in Dutch oven or large saucepan over medium-high heat until hot. Add chicken; cook 5 to 8 minutes, or until lightly browned, stirring frequently. Add onion; cook 3 to 5 minutes, or until onion is crisp-tender.

2. Stir in remaining ingredients. Bring to a boil. Reduce heat to medium; cover and cook 20 to 40 minutes, or until rice is tender and chicken is no longer pink, stirring occasionally.

Yield: 9 (1-cup) servings

Nutrition Information Per Serving

Serving Size: 1 Cup • Calories 210 • Calories from Fat 50 • Total Fat 6 g
Saturated Fat 1 g • Cholesterol 35 mg • Sodium 520 mg • Dietary Fiber 4 g
Dietary Exchanges: 1 Starch, 2 Vegetable, 1 Lean Meat, ½ Fat OR
1 Carbohydrate, 2 Vegetable, 1 Lean Meat, ½ Fat

Recipe Fact

This recipe's a take-off on a well-known Louisiana dish, red beans and rice. We've turned the regional favorite into a soup and have substituted chicken for the usual ham.

Kitchen Tip

For best browning of chicken and other cut-up meat, don't crowd the pan. If necessary, cook in batches.

Make-Ahead Tip

For many stews, soups and chilies, flavors get even better after mellowing for a couple of days. Make (and, of course, refrigerate) this chili up to two days before the serving date, then reheat over low heat.

Chicken Stew Oriental

Prep Time: 40 minutes

Ingredient Substitution

Instead of the chopped bell pepper, try 1 cup of fresh snow pea pods.

Menu Suggestion

This hearty stew is almost a meal in itself! Accompany it with sesame seed hard rolls and finish off with almond cookies and scoops of orange sherbet.

2 tablespoons oil
4 boneless, skinless chicken breast halves, cut into 1-inch pieces
1 garlic clove, minced
2 cups water
1 (8¼-oz.) can pineapple chunks, drained, reserving liquid
⅓ cup uncooked regular long-grain white rice
¼ cup cider vinegar

3 tablespoons brown sugar
2 tablespoons soy sauce
½ teaspoon salt
½ teaspoon finely chopped gingerroot
⅛ teaspoon pepper
½ medium green bell pepper, cut into 1-inch pieces
½ medium red bell pepper, cut into 1-inch pieces
2 tablespoons cornstarch
3 tablespoons water

1. Heat oil in large skillet over medium-high heat until hot. Add chicken and garlic; cook and stir until browned. Stir in 2 cups water, reserved pineapple liquid, rice, vinegar, brown sugar, soy sauce, salt, gingerroot and pepper. Bring to a boil. Reduce heat to low; cover and simmer 12 minutes, or until rice is almost tender.

2. Add bell peppers and pineapple chunks to chicken mixture. Combine cornstarch and 3 tablespoons water; blend well. Add to chicken mixture; cook and stir until thickened and bubbly. Reduce heat to low; cover and simmer an additional 10 to 15 minutes, or until rice is tender and chicken is no longer pink.

Yield: 4 (1¼-cup) servings

Nutrition Information Per Serving
Serving Size: 1¼ Cups • Calories 370 • Calories from Fat 90 • Total Fat 10 g
Saturated Fat 2 g • Cholesterol 75 mg • Sodium 850 mg • Dietary Fiber 1 g
Dietary Exchanges: 1½ Starch, 1 Fruit, 1 Vegetable, 3 Lean Meat OR
2½ Carbohydrate, 1 Vegetable, 3 Lean Meat

Chicken Ratatouille Stew

low-fat

Prep Time: 20 minutes
(Ready in 10 hours 20 minutes)

4 boneless, skinless chicken
　breast halves, cut into
　1-inch pieces
1 (28- to 30-oz.) jar spaghetti
　sauce
1 medium eggplant, peeled,
　coarsely chopped
2 medium tomatoes, coarsely
　chopped

2 small zucchini, sliced
1 medium green bell pepper,
　cut into 1-inch pieces
1 large onion, chopped
3 garlic cloves, minced
1 teaspoon dried basil leaves
1 teaspoon dried oregano
　leaves

1. In 3½- or 4-quart slow cooker, combine all ingredients; mix well.
2. Cover; cook on low setting for 8 to 10 hours, or until chicken is no longer pink.

Yield: 6 (1¾-cup) servings

Nutrition Information Per Serving

Serving Size: 1¾ Cups • Calories 300 • Calories from Fat 80 • Total Fat 9 g
Saturated Fat 2 g • Cholesterol 50 mg • Sodium 750 mg • Dietary Fiber 7 g
Dietary Exchanges: 1 Starch, 3 Vegetable, 2 Lean Meat, ½ Fat OR
1 Carbohydrate, 3 Vegetable, 2 Lean Meat, ½ Fat

Recipe Fact

Ratatouille, a vegetable stew that's a specialty of the French provençal city of Nice, traditionally contains eggplant, zucchini, onion and tomato.

Make-Ahead Tip

Simmer the stew up to two days in advance and refrigerate until serving time. Reheat over low heat.

Make It Special

Just before serving, sprinkle with grated Parmesan or slivers of fresh mozzarella and minced fresh herbs.

Chunky Chicken Chili

low-fat *editor's choice*

Prep Time: 45 minutes

4 boneless, skinless chicken breast halves, cut into bite-sized pieces
1 cup chopped onions
½ cup chopped celery
½ cup chopped carrot
2 garlic cloves, minced
1 cup purchased salsa
1 (28-oz.) can whole tomatoes, undrained, cut up
1 (8-oz.) can tomato sauce
3 teaspoons chili powder
½ teaspoon cumin
1 (15-oz.) can garbanzo beans, drained
1 medium green bell pepper, chopped

1. Spray large nonstick saucepan with nonstick cooking spray. Heat over medium-high heat until hot. Add chicken, onions, celery, carrot and garlic; cook and stir until chicken is no longer pink.

2. Stir in salsa, tomatoes, tomato sauce, chili powder and cumin. Bring to a boil; reduce heat. Cover; simmer 30 minutes, stirring occasionally. Stir in garbanzo beans and bell pepper; simmer until thoroughly heated.

Yield: 6 (1½-cup) servings

> **Nutrition Information Per Serving**
> Serving Size: 1½ Cups • Calories 240 • Calories from Fat 45 • Total Fat 5 g
> Saturated Fat 1 g • Cholesterol 45 mg • Sodium 1020 mg • Dietary Fiber 7 g
> Dietary Exchanges: 1 Starch, 2 Vegetable, 2 Lean Meat OR
> 1 Carbohydrate, 2 Vegetable, 2 Lean Meat

Chunky Chicken Chili

Creole Chicken Gumbo Soup

Recipe Fact

Gumbo, a peppery chicken or meat stew, is a mainstay of Creole cooking. The traditional preparation is thickened with okra or filé powder and thickened further and flavored with a browned flour mixture called roux.

About Bay Leaf

Bay leaf, the dried leaf of the bay laurel tree native to the Mediterranean, adds pungent flavor to soups, stews, dried bean dishes and more. Along with parsley and thyme, bay leaf is a component of the classic French seasoning blend known as **bouquet garni**. Because the edges are sharp, bay leaf should be removed before the soup is served.

1 tablespoon margarine or butter
½ cup chopped green bell pepper
½ cup chopped onion
1 garlic clove, minced
1 tablespoon all-purpose flour
1 cup water
1 (14½-oz.) can ready-to-serve chicken broth
1 (14.5-oz.) can no-salt-added whole tomatoes, undrained, cut up

1 (10-oz.) pkg. frozen cut okra
1½ cups cubed cooked chicken
¼ cup uncooked regular long-grain white rice
¼ teaspoon dried thyme leaves
1 bay leaf
4 to 8 drops hot pepper sauce

1. In large nonstick saucepan, melt margarine over medium heat. Add bell pepper, onion, garlic and flour; cook and stir until flour is light golden brown.
2. Add remaining ingredients. Bring to a boil. Reduce heat to medium-low; cover and cook 10 minutes. Uncover; cook an additional 10 to 15 minutes, or until okra is tender, stirring occasionally. Remove bay leaf.

Yield: 6 (1-cup) servings

Nutrition Information Per Serving
Serving Size: 1 Cup • Calories 180 • Calories from Fat 60 • Total Fat 7 g
Saturated Fat 2 g • Cholesterol 30 mg • Sodium 280 mg • Dietary Fiber 2 g
Dietary Exchanges: ½ Starch, 2 Vegetable, 1 Meat, 1 Fat OR
½ Carbohydrate, 2 Vegetable, 1 Meat, 1 Fat

Italian Chicken Soup

 low-fat

Prep Time: 35 minutes

2 teaspoons oil
4 boneless, skinless chicken
    breast halves, cut into
    1-inch pieces
½ cup chopped onion
¼ cup chopped celery
2 garlic cloves, minced
1 teaspoon dried basil leaves
¼ teaspoon pepper
1 cup water

1 (10½-oz.) can condensed
    chicken broth
1 (14.5-oz.) can stewed
    tomatoes, undrained
1 cup frozen whole kernel corn
1 oz. uncooked vermicelli,
    broken into fourths (⅓ cup)
2 tablespoons grated
    Parmesan cheese

1. Heat oil in large saucepan over medium-high heat until hot. Add chicken; cook and stir until browned. Add onion, celery and garlic; cook and stir until vegetables are crisp-tender. Stir in basil, pepper, water, broth and tomatoes. Bring to a boil. Reduce heat to low; cover and simmer 5 minutes.

2. Stir in corn and vermicelli. Cover; simmer 10 minutes, or until soup is thoroughly heated and vermicelli is tender. Sprinkle each serving with Parmesan cheese.

Yield: 4 (1½-cup) servings

Nutrition Information Per Serving
Serving Size: 1½ Cups • Calories 280 • Calories from Fat 60 • Total Fat 7 g
Saturated Fat 2 g • Cholesterol 75 mg • Sodium 860 mg • Dietary Fiber 2 g
Dietary Exchanges: 1½ Starch, 4 Lean Meat, ½ Fat OR
1½ Carbohydrate, 4 Lean Meat, ½ Fat

About Vermicelli

Vermicelli ("little worms" in Italian) are very thin spaghetti noodles. Other pastas well suited to chicken soup include pastina, orzo, alphabet noodles and ditalini.

Recipe Variation

To stretch the soup to serve more people, add extra broth and other ingredients you might have on hand, such as diced fresh carrot, parsnip slices, canned kidney beans or black beans. Or stir in a cup or two of frozen vegetables and cook long enough to heat through.

Lemony Chicken Soup with Bok Choy

Prep Time: 25 minutes

- **1 tablespoon oil**
- **2 boneless, skinless chicken breast halves, cut into thin strips**
- **1 cup thinly sliced carrots**
- **¹⁄₃ cup diagonally sliced green onions**
- **3 stalks bok choy including leaves, sliced diagonally into ¹⁄₂-inch pieces***
- **¹⁄₂ teaspoon ginger**
- **3 cups water**
- **2 (10¹⁄₂-oz.) cans condensed chicken broth**
- **2 oz. uncooked angel hair pasta, broken into fourths (¹⁄₂ cup)**
- **2 tablespoons lemon juice**

1. Heat oil in Dutch oven or large saucepan over medium-high heat until hot. Add chicken; cook and stir 4 to 5 minutes, or until chicken is no longer pink.

2. Add carrots, green onions, bok choy, ginger, water and broth. Bring to a boil. Reduce heat to low; cover and simmer 5 minutes. Add pasta; cover and simmer 3 to 4 minutes, or until pasta is tender. Stir in lemon juice.

Yield: 6 (1¹⁄₃-cup) servings

***Tip:** Two cups torn fresh spinach can be substituted for the bok choy.

Nutrition Information Per Serving

Serving Size: 1¹⁄₃ Cups • Calories 160 • Calories from Fat 45 • Total Fat 5 g
Saturated Fat 1 g • Cholesterol 25 mg • Sodium 690 mg • Dietary Fiber 2 g
Dietary Exchanges: 2 Vegetable, 2 Lean Meat

Recipe Fact

Pairing lemon and chicken soup has a precedent in the Greek soup classic, **avgolemono** (ahv-goh-LEH-mon-noh).

About Angel Hair Pasta

Angel hair pasta, **capelli d'angelo**, are very thin, quick-cooking strands.

Ingredient Substitution

For variety, substitute chopped spinach for the bok choy.

Menu Suggestion

Serve the soup with crusty rolls or breadsticks for a light, satisfying meal.

Lemony Chicken Soup with Bok Choy

Light Chicken Wild Rice Soup

Prep Time: 30 minutes

2 (14½-oz.) cans ready-to-serve fat-free chicken broth with ⅓ less sodium
3 boneless, skinless chicken breast halves, cut into ¾-inch pieces
1 (6.25-oz.) pkg. quick-cooking long-grain and wild rice mix (with seasoning packet)

¾ cup all-purpose flour
4 cups skim milk
4 slices bacon, cooked until crisp, crumbled
1½ teaspoons diced pimiento
1 tablespoon dry sherry, if desired

1. In Dutch oven or large saucepan, combine broth, chicken, rice and seasoning packet; mix well. Bring to a boil. Reduce heat; cover and simmer 5 to 10 minutes, or until rice is tender.
2. In small bowl, combine flour and 1 cup of the milk; blend until smooth.
3. Add flour mixture, remaining 3 cups milk, bacon, pimiento and sherry to rice mixture; cook and stir over medium heat until soup is thickened and bubbly and chicken is no longer pink. If desired, add salt and pepper to taste.

Yield: 6 (1½-cup) servings

Nutrition Information Per Serving
Serving Size: 1½ Cups • Calories 330 • Calories from Fat 45 • Total Fat 5 g
Saturated Fat 1 g • Cholesterol 45 mg • Sodium 960 mg • Dietary Fiber 1 g
Dietary Exchanges: 3 Starch, 2½ Very Lean Meat OR
3 Carbohydrate, 2½ Very Lean Meat

Mulligatawny Soup

Prep Time: 20 minutes
(Ready in 50 minutes)

3 tablespoons margarine or
 butter
½ cup chopped onion
¼ cup all-purpose flour
1 tablespoon chopped fresh
 parsley
½ teaspoon curry powder
¼ teaspoon nutmeg

⅛ teaspoon pepper
2 whole cloves
3 cups chicken broth
2 cups cubed cooked chicken
1 cup chopped unpeeled apple
½ cup sliced carrot
½ cup sliced celery

1. In large saucepan, melt margarine over medium heat. Add onion; cook and stir until tender. Add flour, parsley, curry powder, nutmeg, pepper and cloves; cook and stir 1 minute, or until smooth and bubbly.
2. Gradually stir in broth; cook until thickened, stirring frequently. Stir in remaining ingredients. Cover; simmer 30 minutes, or until vegetables are crisp-tender. Remove cloves.

Yield: 4 (1¼-cup) servings

Nutrition Information Per Serving

Serving Size: 1¼ Cups • Calories 300 • Calories from Fat 140 • Total Fat 15 g
Saturated Fat 3 g • Cholesterol 60 mg • Sodium 760 mg • Dietary Fiber 2 g
Dietary Exchanges: 1 Starch, 3 Lean Meat, 1 Fat OR
1 Carbohydrate, 3 Lean Meat, 1 Fat

Recipe Fact

This is an easy version of the golden, curry-flavored soup from India.

About Fresh Carrots

If you purchase carrots with the green tops attached, removing the greens before refrigerating the carrots will keep the carrots fresh longer. Although perky tops in the store indicate freshness, the greens actually contribute to loss of crispness in the carrot over time.

Oven Chicken Stew

Prep Time: 30 minutes
(Ready in 2 hours)

Kitchen Tip

For this recipe, you'll need a Dutch oven (a large cooking pot) that is both flameproof and ovenproof. If your Dutch oven is not ovenproof, transfer the mixture to a casserole dish with a cover before baking it.

Ingredient Substitution

In place of the frozen onions, drain a 16-ounce jar of pearl onions and add with the peas.

1 teaspoon salt
½ teaspoon poultry seasoning
½ teaspoon paprika
¼ teaspoon pepper
3 to 3½ lb. cut-up frying chicken
2 tablespoons oil
2 tablespoons tomato paste
1 cup chicken broth

3 medium carrots, cut in half crosswise, quartered lengthwise
1 (16-oz.) pkg. frozen small whole onions
1 (6-oz.) jar whole mushrooms, drained
1 (9-oz.) pkg. frozen sweet peas, thawed
3 tablespoons cornstarch
¼ cup water

1. Heat oven to 350°F. In small bowl, combine salt, poultry seasoning, paprika and pepper; mix well. Rub onto chicken pieces. Heat oil in Dutch oven over medium-high heat until hot. Add chicken; cook until browned on both sides.

2. Remove chicken from Dutch oven; drain and discard drippings. Add tomato paste to Dutch oven; stir in chicken broth. Bring to a boil. Return chicken to Dutch oven. Stir in carrots, onions and mushrooms; cover.

3. Bake at 350°F. for 1½ hours, or until chicken is fork-tender and juices run clear. Stir in peas. Return to stovetop over medium-high heat. In small bowl, combine cornstarch and water; blend until smooth. Stir into chicken mixture; cook until mixture thickens and boils, stirring frequently.

Yield: 6 (1⅓-cup) servings

Nutrition Information Per Serving

Serving Size: 1⅓ Cups • Calories 400 • Calories from Fat 170 • Total Fat 19 g
Saturated Fat 5 g • Cholesterol 90 mg • Sodium 820 mg • Dietary Fiber 6 g
Dietary Exchanges: 1 Starch, 2 Vegetable, 4 Lean Meat, 1 Fat OR
1 Carbohydrate, 2 Vegetable, 4 Lean Meat, 1 Fat

Oven Chicken Stew

Asian Noodle Soup

Prep Time: 15 minutes

About Chinese Noodles

This recipe calls for Chinese noodles—thin wheat noodles that cook very quickly and are eaten hot or cold throughout Asia. Do not substitute crunchy fried chow mein noodles. You may, however, substitute angel hair pasta.

Ingredient Substitution

One cup of frozen regular peas can take the place of the snow peas or sugar snap peas.

Make It Special

Serve the soup in Chinese soup bowls with ceramic spoons, available in Chinese grocery stores and Asian specialty shops. Sprinkle some minced green onion over each serving.

6 cups chicken broth
1½ cups cubed cooked chicken
¾ teaspoon sugar
4 teaspoons soy sauce
2 oz. uncooked thin Chinese wheat noodles, broken into pieces (¾ cup)*

1 cup quartered fresh snow pea pods**
2 green onions, thinly sliced

1. In large saucepan, combine chicken broth, chicken, sugar and soy sauce. Bring to a boil.
2. Add noodles and pea pods. Boil 3 to 5 minutes, or until noodles and pea pods are tender. Sprinkle each serving with green onions.

Yield: 5 (1½-cup) servings

*Tips: Do not use chow mein noodles. Thin Chinese wheat noodles can be found in the oriental section of large supermarkets.

**One 6-oz. pkg. frozen snow pea pods can be substituted for fresh pea pods.

Nutrition Information Per Serving

Serving Size: 1½ Cups • Calories 180 • Calories from Fat 45 • Total Fat 5 g
Saturated Fat 1 g • Cholesterol 35 mg • Sodium 1240 mg • Dietary Fiber 2 g
Dietary Exchanges: ½ Starch, 1 Vegetable, 2 Lean Meat OR
½ Carbohydrate, 1 Vegetable, 2 Lean Meat

Slow-Cooked Chicken and Sausage Stew

Prep Time: 15 minutes
(Ready in 8 hours 15 minutes)

½ cup thinly sliced carrot
2 tablespoons brown sugar
1 teaspoon dry mustard
½ cup ketchup
1 tablespoon vinegar
½ lb. kielbasa sausage, cut into ¼-inch slices
2 boneless, skinless chicken breast halves, cut into thin bite-sized strips

1 medium onion, thinly sliced, separated into rings
1 (16-oz.) can baked beans, undrained
1 (8-oz.) pkg. frozen cut green beans in a pouch, thawed

1. In 3½- or 4-quart slow cooker, combine all ingredients except green beans; mix well. Cover; cook on low setting at least 8 hours, or until chicken is no longer pink and carrot slices are tender.

2. Ten minutes before serving, stir in green beans. Increase heat to high setting; cover and cook 10 minutes, or until green beans are crisp-tender.

Yield: 4 (1½-cup) servings

Nutrition Information Per Serving

Serving Size: 1½ Cups • Calories 460 • Calories from Fat 160 • Total Fat 18 g
Saturated Fat 6 g • Cholesterol 75 mg • Sodium 1520 mg • Dietary Fiber 8 g
Dietary Exchanges: 1 Starch, 1½ Fruit, 2 Vegetable, 3 Medium-Fat Meat, ½ Fat OR
2½ Carbohydrate, 2 Vegetable, 3 Medium-Fat Meat, ½ Fat

About Kielbasa

Kielbasa simply means "sausage" in Polish, but in American usage the term typically refers to a smoked, semi-dry sausage highly seasoned with garlic, black pepper and herbs. It's most often sold precooked, though a butcher may have it available fresh.

Kitchen Tip

When purchasing a slow cooker, look for one with a removable liner to simplify cleanup.

Spicy Chicken Bean Soup

Prep Time: 15 minutes
(Ready in 1 hour 10 minutes)

About Hot Pepper Sauce

The ingredients that make up hot pepper sauce vary by brand. Some consist of nothing more than ground chili peppers in vinegar, while others include additional seasonings. Read the label and experiment with different brands to find your favorite.

Ingredient Substitution

Use any canned or fresh bean in this recipe, or substitute fresh or frozen corn kernels for one of the varieties of beans.

Make It Special

Garnish each serving with a sprinkling of Parmesan cheese, minced fresh parsley and minced green onions.

4 boneless, skinless chicken breast halves, cut into ½-inch pieces
3 cups water
1 (28-oz.) can whole tomatoes, undrained, cut up
1 (8-oz.) pkg. frozen cut green beans in a pouch
1 (9-oz.) pkg. frozen baby lima beans in a pouch
1 (4.5-oz.) can chopped green chiles

1 teaspoon salt
3 teaspoons chili powder
1 teaspoon paprika
¼ teaspoon garlic powder
¼ teaspoon onion powder
¼ teaspoon hot pepper sauce
1 bay leaf
1 (15.5-oz.) can great northern beans, drained

1. In Dutch oven or large saucepan, combine all ingredients except great northern beans. Bring to a boil. Reduce heat to low; cover and simmer 45 to 55 minutes, or until flavors are blended and chicken is no longer pink.
2. Add great northern beans; heat thoroughly. Remove bay leaf.

Yield: 10 (1-cup) servings

Nutrition Information Per Serving
Serving Size: 1 Cup • Calories 110 • Calories from Fat 20 • Total Fat 2 g
Saturated Fat 0 g • Cholesterol 30 mg • Sodium 460 mg • Dietary Fiber 3 g
Dietary Exchanges: 2 Vegetable, 1 Lean Meat

Spicy Chicken Bean Soup

Spicy African Chicken Stew

Prep Time: 20 minutes
(Ready in 55 minutes)

Recipe Fact

This zingy chicken dish shows off the flavors of West Africa—peanuts, tomatoes and hot pepper.

About Peanut Butter

Peanut butters vary in content. The simplest—and often most nutty tasting—are just ground peanuts processed to a spreading consistency. These sometimes are refrigerated; often, the oil separates, requiring you to mix it up before using. Other varieties may have sugar, salt, vegetable oil and other additives.

3 cups cooked rice (cooked as directed on package)
1 tablespoon oil
1 lb. boneless, skinless chicken breasts and thighs, cut into 1-inch pieces
1½ cups chopped onions
2 garlic cloves, minced
1 (28-oz.) can whole tomatoes, undrained, cut up
¼ cup creamy peanut butter

½ teaspoon chili powder
½ teaspoon salt
¼ teaspoon crushed red pepper flakes
½ cup chopped dry-roasted peanuts (unsalted if desired)

1. Heat oil in Dutch oven or large saucepan over medium-high heat until hot. Add chicken, onions and garlic; cook and stir 5 minutes, or until chicken is browned and onions are tender.

2. Stir in tomatoes, peanut butter, chili powder, salt and red pepper flakes. Bring to a boil. Reduce heat; cover and simmer 35 minutes. Serve over rice; sprinkle with peanuts.

Yield: 6 servings

Nutrition Information Per Serving
Serving Size: ⅙ of Recipe • Calories 410 • Calories from Fat 160 • Total Fat 18 g
Saturated Fat 3 g • Cholesterol 45 mg • Sodium 490 mg • Dietary Fiber 4 g
Dietary Exchanges: 2 Starch, 1 Vegetable, 2½ Lean Meat, 2 Fat OR
2 Carbohydrate, 1 Vegetable, 2½ Lean Meat, 2 Fat

White Bean and Chicken Chili

Prep Time: 25 minutes

2 (15.5-oz.) cans great northern beans, drained, rinsed
1½ cups cubed cooked chicken
1 to 2 jalapeño chile peppers, halved, seeded, chopped
1 cup chicken broth

½ teaspoon white pepper
½ cup sour cream
1 tablespoon chopped fresh cilantro
¼ cup purchased guacamole

1. Measure 1 cup of the beans; place in medium saucepan. Mash beans slightly with fork. Add remaining beans, chicken, chile peppers, chicken broth and pepper; bring to a boil.

2. Reduce heat; cover and simmer 15 minutes, stirring occasionally. Stir in sour cream and cilantro. Top each serving with guacamole.

Yield: 4 (1-cup) servings

Nutrition Information Per Serving

Serving Size: 1 Cup • Calories 370 • Calories from Fat 130 • Total Fat 14 g
Saturated Fat 6 g • Cholesterol 60 mg • Sodium 680 mg • Dietary Fiber 9 g
Dietary Exchanges: 2 Starch, 2 Lean Meat, 1 Fat OR
2 Carbohydrate, 2 Lean Meat, 1 Fat

Kitchen Tip

To prevent curdling, do not bring the chili back to a boil once the sour cream has been added.

Make-Ahead Tip

Make and refrigerate the chili up to two days ahead, but do not add the sour cream, cilantro and guacamole until time to reheat and serve.

Menu Suggestion

Serve the chili with warmed flour tortillas and a salad of chopped tomatoes, cucumbers and onion. End the meal with a cool dessert, such as cantaloupe slices topped with a scoop of sherbet.

Vegetable Chicken Chili

Prep Time: 45 minutes

Recipe Fact

Purists argue about what makes a "genuine" chili. Should it contain cubed or ground meat? Beef only or chicken or pork? Tomatoes or beans? Variations abound, with the one common link being chile peppers in some form or other, whether dried, ground, fresh or canned.

Make It Special

Garnish the chili with shredded Cheddar cheese and sour cream or yogurt.

1 tablespoon oil
½ cup chopped onion
1 jalapeño chile pepper, halved, seeded, chopped
1 garlic clove, minced
4 boneless, skinless chicken breast halves, cut into ½-inch pieces
2 teaspoons chili powder
1 teaspoon cumin
½ teaspoon dried oregano leaves
¼ teaspoon pepper
1 medium zucchini, cut in half lengthwise, sliced
¼ cup chili sauce
1 (28-oz.) can whole tomatoes, undrained, cut up
1 (28-oz.) can crushed tomatoes with added puree, undrained
1 (15-oz.) can spicy chili beans, undrained
1 (15-oz.) can black beans, rinsed, drained
1 (11-oz.) can whole kernel corn with red and green peppers, undrained

1. Heat oil in Dutch oven or large saucepan over medium-high heat until hot. Add onion, chile pepper, garlic, chicken, chili powder, cumin, oregano and pepper; cook and stir until chicken is no longer pink.

2. Add remaining ingredients. Bring to a boil. Reduce heat to low; cover and simmer 30 minutes, or until flavors are blended, stirring occasionally.

Yield: 8 (1⅔-cup) servings

Nutrition Information Per Serving

Serving Size: 1⅔ Cups • Calories 270 • Calories from Fat 45 • Total Fat 5 g
Saturated Fat 1 g • Cholesterol 35 mg • Sodium 780 mg • Dietary Fiber 9 g
Dietary Exchanges: 1½ Starch, 2 Vegetable, 2 Lean Meat OR
1½ Carbohydrate, 2 Vegetable, 2 Lean Meat

Vegetable Chicken Chili

Skillet and

Stir-Fry Entrees

Stovetop cooking offers a wealth of wonderful ways to showcase and embellish chicken's mild flavor. All prepared in a standard frying pan, Dutch oven or wok, the easy entrees in this chapter range from imaginative updates of recipe-file favorites to colorful meals made special with herbs and spices from around the world.

Skillet and Stir-Fry Entrees

Previous page: Light Lemon Chicken page 135

Light Lemon Chicken

Prep Time: 20 minutes

30 min. or less • low-fat • editor's choice

4 cups cooked rice (cooked as directed on package)
2 lemons
2 teaspoons cornstarch
1 teaspoon sugar
½ cup chicken broth
2 tablespoons dry sherry
2 tablespoons soy sauce
1 tablespoon oil
4 boneless, skinless chicken breast halves, cut into

¼-inch strips
½ teaspoon salt
⅛ teaspoon pepper
6 to 8 green onions, cut diagonally into 1½-inch pieces
1 medium red bell pepper, cut into ¼-inch strips
1 (4.5-oz.) jar sliced mushrooms, drained

Kitchen Tip

In recipes calling for strips of lemon peel, use only the thin yellow-colored portion of the rind, not the bitter white pith. To remove the colored part, or zest as it's sometimes called, use a sharp paring knife or a vegetable peeler.

Menu Suggestion

Serve the chicken with hot jasmine tea (Chinese tea), carrot sticks and fortune cookies.

1. Cut ⅛-inch thin strips of lemon peel from half of 1 lemon. Set aside. Slice other half and reserve for garnish. Squeeze juice from second lemon. In small bowl, combine cornstarch and sugar. Add 2 tablespoons lemon juice, the broth, sherry and soy sauce; blend well. Set aside.

2. Heat oil in large skillet or wok over medium-high heat until hot. Add chicken; sprinkle with salt and pepper. Cook and stir 3 to 4 minutes, or until chicken is no longer pink. Remove from skillet; cover to keep warm.

3. Add green onions, bell pepper and mushrooms to skillet. Cook and stir 1 minute. Add lemon juice mixture to vegetables; cook and stir 1 to 2 minutes, or until thickened. Return chicken to skillet; add lemon strips. Cook and stir 1 minute. Serve with rice. Garnish with lemon slices.

Yield: 4 servings

Nutrition Information Per Serving

Serving Size: ¼ of Recipe • Calories 430 • Calories from Fat 60 • Total Fat 7 g
Saturated Fat 2 g • Cholesterol 75 mg • Sodium 1090 mg • Dietary Fiber 3 g
Dietary Exchanges: 3 Starch, 2 Vegetable, 2½ Lean Meat OR
3 Carbohydrate, 2 Vegetable, 2½ Lean Meat

Braised Chicken and Italian Vegetables

Prep Time: 30 minutes
(Ready in 1 hour 20 minutes)

Recipe Fact

Braising is a long, slow cooking process that tenderizes meats and develops flavors. First the food is browned in hot fat, then it is cooked tightly covered in a small amount of liquid.

About Eggplant

The purple eggplant commonly found in U.S. markets doesn't resemble an egg, but a small white-skinned Asian variety does. Japanese eggplant is also purple, but is more slender and slightly sweeter than the larger kind. Choose eggplants that feel heavy for their size.

About Cornstarch

While some purists turn up their noses at "old-fashioned" sauces thickened with cornstarch, the fact remains that cornstarch adds body without fat. For best results, dissolve the cornstarch in a small amount of liquid, then pour the dissolved mixture into the sauce to be thickened.

2 tablespoons olive oil or vegetable oil
1 small eggplant, cut into $\frac{1}{2}$-inch cubes
1 medium zucchini, sliced
1 medium red bell pepper, cut into $\frac{1}{2}$-inch squares
1 small onion, chopped
2 garlic cloves, minced
3 to $3\frac{1}{2}$ lb. cut-up or quartered frying chicken, skin removed, if desired

$\frac{1}{2}$ teaspoon salt
$\frac{1}{4}$ teaspoon pepper
2 tablespoons olive oil or vegetable oil
$\frac{1}{2}$ teaspoon dried thyme leaves
1 teaspoon dried oregano leaves
1 (14.5- or 16-oz.) can stewed tomatoes, undrained, cut up
$1\frac{1}{2}$ teaspoons cornstarch

1. Heat 2 tablespoons oil in large skillet or Dutch oven over medium-high heat until hot. Add eggplant, zucchini, bell pepper, onion and garlic; cook and stir 8 to 10 minutes, or until tender. Place vegetables in bowl; set aside.

2. Sprinkle chicken with salt and pepper. Heat 2 tablespoons oil in same skillet. Brown chicken in hot oil; drain. Add thyme, oregano and tomatoes. Bring to a boil. Reduce heat to low; cover and simmer 45 to 50 minutes, or until chicken is fork-tender and juices run clear.

3. With slotted spoon, place chicken on serving platter. Spoon 1 tablespoon tomato liquid from skillet into small bowl. Add cornstarch; blend until smooth. Add vegetable mixture to skillet. Stir in cornstarch mixture. Bring to a boil. Reduce heat; simmer uncovered 5 minutes. Pour over chicken.

Yield: 6 servings

Nutrition Information Per Serving

Serving Size: $\frac{1}{6}$ of Recipe • Calories 280 • Calories from Fat 140 • Total Fat 16 g
Saturated Fat 3 g • Cholesterol 75 mg • Sodium 430 mg • Dietary Fiber 2 g
Dietary Exchanges: 2 Vegetable, 3 Lean Meat, $1\frac{1}{2}$ Fat

---

Braised Chicken Paprikash

Prep Time: 1 hour

3 to 3½ lb. cut-up frying
   chicken, skin removed
3 tablespoons all-purpose flour
3 tablespoons margarine or
   butter
1 (12-oz.) jar chicken gravy
½ cup finely chopped onion
½ cup thinly sliced red or
   green bell pepper

1 tablespoon paprika
8 oz. (4 cups) uncooked wide
   egg noodles
1 tablespoon margarine or
   butter
½ cup soft bread crumbs
½ cup sour cream
⅛ teaspoon pepper

1. Sprinkle chicken with flour. In large skillet, melt 3 tablespoons margarine over medium-high heat. Add chicken; cook 4 to 5 minutes on each side, or until light golden brown.

2. In small bowl, combine gravy, onion, bell pepper and paprika; pour over chicken. Cover; cook over low heat 40 to 45 minutes, or until chicken is fork-tender and juices run clear, stirring occasionally. If desired, skim off fat.

3. Meanwhile, cook noodles to desired doneness as directed on package. Drain; keep warm.

4. In small saucepan, melt 1 tablespoon margarine over medium heat. Add bread crumbs; cook and stir until lightly browned. Set aside.

5. Stir sour cream and pepper into chicken and gravy. Cook over low heat until thoroughly heated, stirring constantly. DO NOT BOIL. Serve chicken over hot cooked noodles; top with gravy. Sprinkle with bread crumbs.

Yield: 6 servings

Nutrition Information Per Serving

Serving Size: ⅙ of Recipe • Calories 490 • Calories from Fat 210 • Total Fat 23 g
Saturated Fat 7 g • Cholesterol 120 mg • Sodium 530 mg • Dietary Fiber 2 g
Dietary Exchanges: 2 Starch, 1½ Vegetable, 3½ Lean Meat, 2 Fat OR
2 Carbohydrate, 1½ Vegetable, 3½ Lean Meat, 2 Fat

Recipe Fact

Chicken paprikash, a signature dish of Hungary, combines poultry with flavorful Hungarian paprika and sour cream.

About Paprika

Paprika—dried ground hot or sweet chile peppers—ranges from being a decorative sprinkle with virtually no flavor to a pungent culinary accent. Hungarian paprika (usually labeled "Hungarian") is considered by many to be the best quality; look for it in specialty or ethnic markets, and refrigerate it to maintain freshness.

Kitchen Tip

Once the sour cream goes into the pot, watch carefully to make sure that the liquid doesn't boil, or the sour cream will curdle. Allow it to just heat through.

Chicken Almond Ding

Prep Time: 25 minutes

About Water Chestnuts

Water chestnuts—edible tubers that grow under-water—add mild crunch to cold salads and hot entrees. They're available canned, either whole or sliced. Fresh water chest-nuts, available in Chinese markets, are another thing altogether, endowed with a much crisper texture and an incredible natural sweet-ness. Peel them before using.

Kitchen Tip

When cooking in a wok, add the ingredients a small amount at a time in the center of the wok. As they begin to cook, move them up the sides of the wok and stir the next batch of ingredients into the middle.

4 cups cooked rice (cooked as directed on package)
1 cup chicken broth
2 tablespoons cornstarch
2 tablespoons soy sauce
1 tablespoon rice vinegar
1 teaspoon sugar
1/4 teaspoon salt, if desired
1 tablespoon oil
2 garlic cloves, minced
1/2 cup slivered almonds
4 boneless, skinless chicken breast halves, cut into 1/2-inch pieces
1 medium red bell pepper, cut into 3/4-inch pieces
1 cup fresh snow pea pods, trimmed, cut diagonally in half
1 (8-oz.) can sliced water chestnuts, drained
2 cups chopped Chinese (napa) cabbage

1. In small bowl, combine broth, cornstarch, soy sauce, vinegar, sugar and salt; mix well. Set aside.

2. Heat oil in large skillet or wok over medium-high heat until hot. Add garlic, almonds and chicken; cook and stir 3 to 4 minutes, or until chicken is no longer pink and almonds are golden brown.

3. Add bell pepper; cook and stir 2 to 3 minutes. Add pea pods and water chestnuts; cook and stir 3 to 4 minutes, or until vegetables are crisp-tender. Add cabbage and cornstarch mixture; cook and stir until sauce is thick-ened and bubbly. Serve over rice.

Yield: 4 servings

Nutrition Information Per Serving
Serving Size: 1/4 of Recipe • Calories 560 • Calories from Fat 140 • Total Fat 15 g
Saturated Fat 2 g • Cholesterol 70 mg • Sodium 940 mg • Dietary Fiber 5 g
Dietary Exchanges: 4 Starch, 1 Vegetable, 3 Lean Meat, 1 Fat OR
4 Carbohydrate, 1 Vegetable, 3 Lean Meat, 1 Fat

Chicken Almond Ding

Chicken Cacciatore

Prep Time: 1 hour

Kitchen Tip

For best browning, use a skillet large enough to hold the chicken in a single layer, or fry it in batches.

Menu Suggestion

Serve the cacciatore over hot pasta and accompany with Italian beans, garlic bread and a big tossed salad. For dessert, offer store-bought miniature Italian cannoli and cappuccino. To approximate cappuccino without a steam-driven espresso maker, brew hot coffee in your usual fashion, but make it extra strong. Heat 8 ounces of milk in a 16-ounce microwave-safe glass measuring cup in the microwave for 2 to 3 minutes on HIGH. Whip the hot milk with a small whisk to create foam. Pour it into cups half filled with the strong coffee. Sprinkle the top with a mixture of sugar and cinnamon or unsweetened cocoa powder, if desired.

¼ cup all-purpose flour
3 to 3½ lb. cut-up frying chicken, skin removed
2 tablespoons oil
1 (14.5- or 16-oz.) can whole tomatoes, undrained, cut up
1 medium onion, sliced
1 medium green bell pepper, sliced
1 teaspoon dried Italian seasoning
½ teaspoon sugar
½ teaspoon salt
⅛ teaspoon pepper

Stovetop Directions: 1. Place flour in shallow bowl; coat chicken pieces in flour. Heat oil in large skillet over medium-high heat until hot. Add chicken; brown well on all sides. Drain and discard oil from skillet. Add remaining ingredients to skillet. Bring to a boil.
2. Reduce heat to low; cover and simmer 30 to 40 minutes, or until chicken is fork-tender and juices run clear, stirring occasionally. If desired, serve over hot cooked pasta.

Yield: 6 servings

Microwave Directions: 1. Omit flour and oil. Arrange chicken in 12 × 8-inch (2-quart) microwave-safe dish. In medium bowl, combine remaining ingredients; pour over chicken. Cover with microwave-safe plastic wrap.
2. Microwave on HIGH for 22 to 26 minutes, or until chicken is fork-tender and juices run clear, rotating dish ½ turn and spooning sauce over chicken once during cooking. If desired, serve over hot cooked pasta.

Nutrition Information Per Serving
Serving Size: ⅙ of Recipe • Calories 240 • Calories from Fat 100 • Total Fat 11 g
Saturated Fat 2 g • Cholesterol 75 mg • Sodium 370 mg • Dietary Fiber 1 g
Dietary Exchanges: 2 Vegetable, 3½ Lean Meat

Chicken and Fettuccine Primavera

Prep Time: 25 minutes

6 oz. uncooked fettuccine
1 tablespoon olive oil or vegetable oil
4 boneless, skinless chicken breast halves, cut into thin strips
1 (14.5-oz.) can Italian-style tomatoes with olive oil, garlic and spices, undrained
½ teaspoon fennel seed

¼ teaspoon salt
⅛ teaspoon ground red pepper (cayenne)
1 cup coarsely chopped green bell pepper
2 cups sliced yellow summer squash
1 oz. (¼ cup) shredded fresh Parmesan cheese, if desired

1. Cook fettuccine to desired doneness as directed on package. Drain; cover to keep warm.

2. Meanwhile, heat oil in large skillet or Dutch oven over medium-high heat until hot. Add chicken strips; cook and stir until browned. Stir in tomatoes, fennel seed, salt and ground red pepper. Bring to a boil. Reduce heat to medium; cook 2 to 3 minutes.

3. Stir in bell pepper and summer squash; cook an additional 4 to 6 minutes, or until vegetables are crisp-tender and chicken is no longer pink, stirring occasionally. Stir in fettuccine; cook an additional 2 to 4 minutes, or until thoroughly heated, stirring frequently. Sprinkle with Parmesan cheese.

Yield: 4 (1¾-cup) servings

Nutrition Information Per Serving
Serving Size: 1¾ Cups • Calories 410 • Calories from Fat 110 • Total Fat 12 g
Saturated Fat 3 g • Cholesterol 110 mg • Sodium 760 mg • Dietary Fiber 4 g
Dietary Exchanges: 2 Starch, 2 Vegetable, 3½ Lean Meat OR
2 Carbohydrate, 2 Vegetable, 3½ Lean Meat

Recipe Fact

Primavera, Italian for "spring," here refers to the colorful mixture of vegetables. Our version is lower in fat than many traditional renditions, which negate the healthy attributes of the vegetables by drowning them in fat-laden heavy-cream sauces.

About Fennel Seed

Fennel seed has a distinctive licorice taste and is a key flavor in Italian sausage. In fact, to approximate the flavor of Italian sausage while keeping a low-fat profile, sprinkle fennel seeds into your favorite soup, stew or spaghetti sauce.

About Fettuccine

Fettuccine noodles resemble flattened spaghetti noodles and provide plenty of surface area for sauce to cling to. You can substitute any available pasta.

Chicken Breasts Florentine

Prep Time: 20 minutes

1 (9-oz.) pkg. frozen spinach in a pouch
3 tablespoons butter, melted
4 boneless, skinless chicken breast halves
⅓ cup plain bread crumbs
¼ teaspoon dried basil leaves
2 tablespoons oil
2 oz. (½ cup) shredded mozzarella cheese

1. Cook spinach as directed on package; squeeze to drain. Stir in butter; set aside.

2. Meanwhile, place 1 chicken breast half between 2 pieces of plastic wrap or waxed paper. Working from center, gently pound chicken with flat side of meat mallet or rolling pin until about ¼ inch thick; remove wrap. Repeat with remaining chicken breast halves. In shallow bowl, combine bread crumbs and basil. Coat chicken breasts with crumb mixture.

3. Heat oil in large skillet over medium-high heat until hot. Add chicken breasts; cook 5 to 7 minutes on each side, or until lightly browned, fork-tender and juices run clear. Reduce heat to low. Spoon cooked spinach evenly over each chicken breast half; sprinkle with cheese. Cover; cook until cheese is melted.

Yield: 4 servings

Nutrition Information Per Serving

Serving Size: ¼ of Recipe • Calories 370 • Calories from Fat 200 • Total Fat 22 g
Saturated Fat 9 g • Cholesterol 105 mg • Sodium 450 mg • Dietary Fiber 1 g
Dietary Exchanges: 2 Vegetable, 4 Lean Meat, 2 Fat

Chicken and Bean Skillet Supper

Prep Time: 30 minutes

4 slices bacon, cut into ½-inch pieces

2 boneless, skinless chicken breast halves, cut into 1-inch pieces

4 boneless, skinless chicken thighs, cut into 1-inch pieces

1 cup chopped onions

1 cup chopped green bell pepper

½ cup purchased thick and chunky salsa

½ teaspoon dried thyme leaves

1 (16-oz.) can baked beans, undrained

1 (15.5-oz.) can dark red kidney beans, drained

1 (15.5-oz.) can great northern beans, drained

1. In large skillet or Dutch oven, cook bacon over medium heat until crisp. Drain, reserving 3 tablespoons drippings in skillet. Add chicken, onions and bell pepper; cook and stir until chicken is browned.

2. Stir in remaining ingredients. Bring to a boil. Reduce heat to low; simmer 15 to 20 minutes, or until chicken is no longer pink, stirring occasionally.

Yield: 6 (1⅓-cup) servings

Nutrition Information Per Serving

Serving Size: 1⅓ Cups • Calories 390 • Calories from Fat 140 • Total Fat 15 g
Saturated Fat 5 g • Cholesterol 70 mg • Sodium 890 mg • Dietary Fiber 9 g
Dietary Exchanges: 2 Starch, 1 Vegetable, 3 Lean Meat, 1 Fat OR
2 Carbohydrate, 1 Vegetable, 3 Lean Meat, 1 Fat

Healthy Hint

To reduce the fat to 8 grams per serving, cook the bacon in the microwave, sandwiched between sheets of microwave-safe paper towels. Instead of browning the chicken and vegetables in the bacon drippings, coat the pan with nonstick cooking spray.

Make-Ahead Tip

The flavors in this hearty one-dish meal will blend as they sit. Make the recipe up to two days before serving and refrigerate it until needed. Reheat over low heat.

Chicken Curry Stuffed Potatoes

Prep Time: 20 minutes
(Ready in 55 minutes)

About Curry Powder

Curry powder, essential to the cuisine of India, is not a single spice but a blend that varies from cook to cook and from brand to brand. Commercial mixtures usually include cumin, turmeric, ginger, coriander seeds and pepper, and sometimes also cardamom, cinnamon, cloves, mace and more.

Healthy Hint

To save 15 grams fat and 110 calories per serving, use nonfat sour cream and reduced-fat Cheddar in place of regular.

4 medium baking potatoes	¼ cup chopped red bell pepper
1 cup chicken broth	1 cup sour cream
2 tablespoons all-purpose flour	2 teaspoons lemon juice
½ teaspoon curry powder	1 cup chopped cooked chicken
¼ teaspoon onion salt	2 oz. (½ cup) shredded Cheddar cheese
1 tablespoon oil	
2 cups fresh broccoli florets or frozen cut broccoli	

Oven Directions: 1. Heat oven to 400°F. Pierce potatoes with fork. Bake at 400°F. for 45 to 55 minutes, or until tender.

2. Meanwhile, in small bowl using wire whisk, blend broth, flour, curry powder and onion salt. Heat oil in large skillet over medium-high heat until hot. Gradually add frozen broccoli and bell pepper; cook and stir 5 to 7 minutes, or until broccoli is crisp-tender. Reduce heat to medium.

3. Gradually stir in chicken broth mixture; cook and stir until sauce is thickened and bubbly. Remove from heat. Stir in sour cream, lemon juice and chicken. Cook over low heat 2 minutes, or until thoroughly heated.

4. To serve, cut potatoes in half lengthwise, cutting to but not through bottom of potatoes. Mash slightly with fork. Place potatoes on 4 individual plates; spoon chicken mixture over hot potatoes. Sprinkle with cheese.

Yield: 4 servings

Microwave Directions: 1. Pierce potatoes with fork; place on microwave-safe roasting rack. Microwave on HIGH for 5 minutes; turn potatoes. Microwave on HIGH for an additional 5 to 7 minutes, or until tender; cover to keep warm.

2. In 2-quart microwave-safe casserole, cook broccoli with bell peppers as directed on broccoli package; drain.

3. In 4-cup microwave-safe measuring cup using wire whisk, blend broth, flour, curry powder and onion salt. Microwave on HIGH for $3\frac{1}{2}$ to $4\frac{1}{2}$ minutes, or until mixture boils and thickens, stirring once halfway through cooking. Stir in sour cream, lemon juice and chicken. Add to cooked broccoli; mix well. Microwave on HIGH for 3 to 4 minutes, or until thoroughly heated, stirring once halfway through cooking. Serve as directed above.

Nutrition Information Per Serving

Serving Size: $\frac{1}{4}$ of Recipe • Calories 430 • Calories from Fat 190 • Total Fat 21 g
Saturated Fat 12 g • Cholesterol 75 mg • Sodium 480 mg • Dietary Fiber 4 g
Dietary Exchanges: 2 Starch, 2 Vegetable, 2 Lean Meat, 3 Fat OR
2 Carbohydrate, 2 Vegetable, 2 Lean Meat, 3 Fat

Chicken Curry Stuffed Potatoes

Chicken Kiev

Prep Time: 40 minutes

Recipe Fact

Chicken Kiev, a favorite banquet dish, consists of breaded chicken breasts rolled around a lump of butter and browned in a frying pan. The surprise comes at the table, when piercing the roll with fork and knife releases a flavorful squirt of melted butter.

Kitchen Tip

Make sure the butter is very cold—even frozen—before frying, so it will melt at the right time and not leak out before frying is complete.

Make It Special

Soften the butter and mix it with minced fresh herbs. Shape the butter into a log shape and chill until firm. Put a slice of the herbed butter into each chicken breast. Garnish each serving with a sprig of the same herb used for the butter. (Pass any extra herbed butter at the table with dinner rolls.)

8 boneless, skinless chicken breast halves
¼ teaspoon salt
⅛ teaspoon pepper
1 tablespoon finely chopped fresh parsley
1½ teaspoons chopped fresh chives or ½ teaspoon dried tarragon leaves

1 stick (¼ lb.) cold butter or margarine
¼ cup all-purpose flour
1 egg, slightly beaten
½ cup plain bread crumbs
Oil for frying

1. Place 1 chicken breast half between 2 pieces of plastic wrap or waxed paper. Working from center, gently pound chicken with flat side of meat mallet or rolling pin until about ⅛ inch thick; remove wrap. Repeat with remaining chicken breast halves.

2. Sprinkle chicken with salt, pepper, parsley and chives. Cut cold butter into quarters lengthwise and then in half crosswise to make 8 pieces. Place 1 piece of butter on each chicken breast half. Fold in sides; roll up jelly-roll fashion, pressing ends to seal. Coat chicken with flour; dip in egg. Roll in bread crumbs. Cover; refrigerate until ready to fry.

3. About 15 minutes before serving, heat 1½ to 2 inches oil in medium skillet over medium heat until hot. Fry chicken rolls about 10 minutes, or until chicken is golden brown, fork-tender and juices run clear, turning to brown all sides.

Yield: 8 servings

Nutrition Information Per Serving

Serving Size: ⅛ of Recipe • Calories 320 • Calories from Fat 170 • Total Fat 19 g
Saturated Fat 9 g • Cholesterol 130 mg • Sodium 310 mg • Dietary Fiber 0 g
Dietary Exchanges: ½ Starch, 4 Lean Meat, 1½ Fat OR
½ Carbohydrate, 4 Lean Meat, 1½ Fat

Creamed Chicken with Sun-Dried Tomatoes

Prep Time: 20 minutes

1 (9-oz.) pkg. uncooked
  refrigerated spinach
  fettuccine
2 tablespoons oil
2 boneless, skinless chicken
  breast halves, cut into thin
  strips
1 cup chopped leek
2 garlic cloves, minced
½ cup coarsely chopped sun-
  dried tomatoes packed in
  oil, drained

¼ cup finely chopped cooked
  ham
½ teaspoon dried oregano
  leaves
1 cup chicken broth
1 tablespoon cornstarch
⅔ cup half-and-half

1. In large saucepan, cook fettuccine to desired doneness as directed on package. Drain; cover to keep warm.
2. Meanwhile, heat oil in large skillet over medium-high heat until hot. Add chicken, leeks and garlic; cook and stir 4 to 5 minutes, or until chicken is no longer pink. Add tomatoes, ham, oregano and broth. Bring to a boil. Reduce heat; cover and simmer 5 minutes.
3. In small bowl, combine cornstarch and half-and-half; blend until smooth. Gradually stir into mixture in skillet. Cook and stir over medium-high heat until mixture boils and thickens, stirring constantly. Serve over fettuccine.

Yield: 4 servings

Nutrition Information Per Serving
Serving Size: ¼ of Recipe • Calories 460 • Calories from Fat 160 • Total Fat 18 g
Saturated Fat 5 g • Cholesterol 100 mg • Sodium 450 mg • Dietary Fiber 4 g
Dietary Exchanges: 3 Starch, 1 Vegetable, 2 Lean Meat, 2 Fat OR
3 Carbohydrate, 1 Vegetable, 2 Lean Meat, 2 Fat

About Leeks

The leek, a mild member of the onion family, resembles a fat, over-grown scallion. Since it tends to hold a lot of dirt within the leaves, wash it thoroughly: Trim off the root end, then cut the leek in half lengthwise and rinse completely, separating the layers to make sure all the grit is removed.

Healthy Hint

To lower the fat in this recipe a little bit, choose dry sun-dried tomatoes instead of the oil-packed variety. To reconstitute the dried tomatoes, place them in a glass measuring cup or bowl and add hot water to cover. Microwave on HIGH for a minute, then let them stand for about 5 minutes, or until softened. Squeeze out most of the liquid, chop the tomatoes and add as directed.

Chicken Marengo

Prep Time: 40 minutes

1 tablespoon olive oil or
    vegetable oil
4 bone-in chicken breast
    halves, skin removed
1 tablespoon all-purpose flour
½ teaspoon dried basil leaves
¼ teaspoon garlic powder
⅛ teaspoon pepper
½ cup dry white wine or
    chicken broth

2 tablespoons tomato paste
2 (14.5- or 16-oz.) cans regular
    or Italian whole tomatoes,
    well drained, cut up
½ cup coarsely chopped green
    bell pepper
1 medium onion, cut into 8 thin
    wedges
¼ cup halved or sliced pitted
    ripe olives

1. Heat oil in large skillet over medium-high heat until hot. Add chicken breast halves; cook until browned on all sides.
2. In medium bowl, combine flour, basil, garlic powder, pepper, wine and tomato paste; blend until smooth. Stir in tomatoes. Move chicken to side of skillet; add tomato mixture. Place chicken, meaty side up, in tomato mixture. Bring to a boil. Reduce heat to medium low; cover and cook 10 minutes, stirring occasionally.
3. Turn chicken; stir in bell pepper and onion. Cover; cook an additional 8 to 10 minutes, or until chicken is fork-tender and juices run clear, stirring occasionally. Stir in olives.

Yield: 4 servings

Nutrition Information Per Serving
Serving Size: ¼ of Recipe • Calories 280 • Calories from Fat 70 • Total Fat 8 g
Saturated Fat 1 g • Cholesterol 75 mg • Sodium 230 mg • Dietary Fiber 3 g
Dietary Exchanges: ½ Starch, 2 Vegetable, 3½ Lean Meat OR
½ Carbohydrate, 2 Vegetable, 3½ Lean Meat

Recipe Fact

Said to have been created by Napoleon's chef after the 1800 Battle of Marengo, this famous dish combines chicken with tomatoes, olives and white wine.

Menu Suggestion

Serve the chicken over rice or pasta, along with a glass of dry white wine (since you need to use some in the recipe itself). Accompany with baked acorn squash.

Chicken Marengo

Chicken Risotto

Prep Time: 25 minutes

Recipe Fact

This recipe greatly speeds preparation of risotto. For the classic Italian dish, short-grained (nearly round) Arborio rice cooks in a skillet and the cook adds liquid a little bit at a time, stirring constantly until the liquid is absorbed, then adding more liquid. The method results in a creamy-textured rice dish.

2 tablespoons olive oil or vegetable oil
4 boneless, skinless chicken breast halves, cut into ¾-inch pieces
½ cup chicken broth
⅓ cup dry white wine
⅛ teaspoon pepper

1 (9-oz.) pkg. frozen mixed vegetables in a pouch
1 cup uncooked instant white rice
½ cup sliced green onions
2 to 4 tablespoons grated Parmesan cheese

Stovetop Directions: 1. Heat oil in large skillet over medium-high heat until hot. Add chicken; cook and stir 2 to 4 minutes, or until lightly browned. Drain. Add broth, wine, pepper and vegetables. Bring to a boil.

2. Reduce heat to low; cover and simmer 5 minutes, or until chicken is no longer pink and vegetables are crisp-tender. Stir in rice and green onions. Remove from heat. Cover; let stand 5 minutes. Sprinkle with Parmesan cheese.

Yield: 4 servings

Microwave Directions: 1. Omit oil. Place chicken in 2-quart microwave-safe casserole; cover tightly. Microwave on HIGH for 5 to 6 minutes, or until no longer pink on outside, stirring once halfway through cooking. Drain. Stir in broth, wine, pepper and vegetables; cover tightly.

2. Microwave on HIGH for 6 to 7 minutes, or until chicken is no longer pink in center and vegetables are crisp-tender, stirring once halfway through cooking. Stir in rice and onions. Cover; let stand 5 minutes. Sprinkle with Parmesan cheese.

Nutrition Information Per Serving
Serving Size: ¼ of Recipe • Calories 370 • Calories from Fat 110 • Total Fat 12 g
Saturated Fat 3 g • Cholesterol 75 mg • Sodium 350 mg • Dietary Fiber 3 g
Dietary Exchanges: 2 Starch, 4 Lean Meat OR 2 Carbohydrate, 4 Lean Meat

Chicken with Pasta and Pesto

• 30 min. or less • editor's choice

Prep Time: 20 minutes

5 oz. (2 cups) uncooked
   medium shell pasta
1 tablespoon oil
4 boneless, skinless chicken
   breast halves, cut into
   1-inch pieces

1 (14-oz.) can artichoke hearts,
   drained, quartered
½ cup purchased pesto
½ cup chopped tomato
1 oz. (¼ cup) shredded fresh
   Parmesan cheese

1. Cook pasta to desired doneness as directed on package. Drain; cover to keep warm.

2. Meanwhile, heat oil in large skillet over medium-high heat until hot. Add chicken; cook and stir 4 to 5 minutes, or until browned and no longer pink. Stir in artichoke hearts, pesto and pasta. Cook an additional 1 to 2 minutes, or until thoroughly heated, stirring constantly. Sprinkle with tomato and Parmesan cheese.

Yield: 4 (1½-cup) servings

Nutrition Information Per Serving

Serving Size: 1½ Cups • Calories 440 • Calories from Fat 140 • Total Fat 16 g
Saturated Fat 4 g • Cholesterol 80 mg • Sodium 340 mg • Dietary Fiber 5 g
Dietary Exchanges: 2 Starch, 1 Vegetable, 4 Lean Meat, 1 Fat OR
2 Carbohydrate, 1 Vegetable, 4 Lean Meat, 1 Fat

About Pesto

Pesto, an uncooked sauce for pasta, contains copious amounts of fresh sweet basil crushed with a mortar and pestle (or chopped in a food processor) with olive oil, garlic, pine nuts and Parmesan cheese.

Menu Suggestion

For an Italian-accented summer supper, start the meal with prosciutto and slices of fresh melon. Serve the main course with an Italian white wine, tossed salad and garlic bread. For dessert, Italian ice!

Country Captain Chicken

Prep Time: 1 hour 15 minutes

Recipe Fact

This dish gets its name from a British army captain who is said to have brought the recipe back to England from his station in India. It blends the cuisines of the two countries, combining ingredients typical in British cooking—chicken, onions and tomato—with common Indian ingredients—curry and raisins or currants. The finished dish is sprinkled with toasted almonds and usually served with rice.

Recipe Variation

Substitute 2 cups of orange juice for the tomatoes. Garnish the chicken with shredded coconut (toasted in a skillet) and pass along a dish of sautéed bananas (whole or halved bananas browned in butter in a skillet until heated through and softened).

3 cups cooked rice (cooked as directed on package)
¼ cup all-purpose flour
½ teaspoon salt
¼ teaspoon pepper
3 to 3½ lb. cut-up frying chicken, skin removed, if desired
2 tablespoons oil
½ cup chopped onion
¼ cup raisins
2 tablespoons chopped fresh
parsley
1½ teaspoons curry powder
½ teaspoon salt
1 medium green bell pepper, cut into ½-inch pieces
1 garlic clove, minced
1 (14.5- to 16-oz.) can whole tomatoes, undrained, cut up
¼ cup slivered almonds, toasted*

1. In plastic bag, combine flour, ½ teaspoon salt and pepper; shake to mix. Add chicken pieces, 1 or 2 at a time, to mixture in bag; shake to coat chicken.

2. Heat oil in large skillet or Dutch oven over medium-high heat until hot. Add chicken; cook until browned on all sides; drain. Add remaining ingredients except rice and almonds to chicken in skillet. Bring to a boil. Reduce heat to low; cover and simmer 50 to 60 minutes, or until chicken is fork-tender and juices run clear, rearranging chicken pieces once or twice during cooking. Serve chicken mixture over rice; sprinkle with almonds.

Yield: 6 servings

*Tip: To toast almonds, spread on cookie sheet; bake at 350°F. for 5 to 7 minutes, or until golden brown, stirring occasionally. Or, spread almonds in thin layer in microwave-safe pie pan. Microwave on HIGH for 4 to 7 minutes, or until golden brown, stirring frequently.

Nutrition Information Per Serving

Serving Size: ⅙ of Recipe • Calories 420 • Calories from Fat 130 • Total Fat 14 g
Saturated Fat 3 g • Cholesterol 75 mg • Sodium 590 mg • Dietary Fiber 3 g
Dietary Exchanges: 3 Starch, 3½ Lean Meat OR 3 Carbohydrate, 3½ Lean Meat

---

Country Captain Chicken

Citrus Chicken with Peppers

Prep Time: 20 minutes

Recipe Variation

For a special summer dish, dice the bell peppers instead of cutting them into strips; proceed as directed. A minute or two before serving time, add 2 sliced peeled fresh peaches or nectarines and stir until the fruit is heated through and slightly softened.

Make It Special

Garnish each plate with a thin slice of fresh orange, a thin slice of fresh lime and a couple of fresh cherries.

Menu Suggestion

Serve the chicken with brown rice and steamed green beans or sugar snap peas, followed by angel food cake drizzled with chocolate sauce and garnished with fresh berries.

4 boneless, skinless chicken breast halves	2 tablespoons lime juice
	2 tablespoons honey
1 medium red bell pepper, cut into strips	½ teaspoon paprika
	¼ teaspoon salt
1 medium green bell pepper, cut into strips	Dash pepper
	1 tablespoon cornstarch
⅓ cup orange juice	2 tablespoons water

Stovetop Directions: 1. Place chicken breast halves in large skillet. Arrange bell pepper strips around chicken. In small bowl, combine orange juice, lime juice, honey, paprika, salt and pepper; blend well. Pour over chicken and peppers. Bring to a boil; reduce heat. Cover; simmer 8 to 10 minutes, or until chicken is fork-tender and juices run clear. Using slotted spoon, transfer chicken and peppers to serving plate; cover to keep warm.
2. In small bowl, combine cornstarch and water; blend until smooth. Stir into hot liquid in skillet. Cook over medium heat until mixture thickens and boils, stirring constantly. Spoon over chicken and peppers.

Yield: 4 servings

Microwave Directions: 1. Place chicken breast halves in 12 × 8-inch (2-quart) microwave-safe dish. Arrange bell pepper strips around chicken. In small bowl, combine orange juice, lime juice, honey, paprika, salt and pepper; blend well. Pour over chicken and peppers. Cover with microwave-safe plastic wrap.
2. Microwave on HIGH for 8 to 12 minutes, until chicken is no longer pink, rearranging chicken and spooning sauce over it once halfway through cooking. Using slotted spoon, transfer chicken and peppers to serving plate; cover to keep warm.

3. In small bowl, combine cornstarch and water; blend until smooth. Stir into hot liquid in dish. Microwave on HIGH for 1½ to 3 minutes, or until thickened, stirring once during cooking. Spoon over chicken and peppers.

Nutrition Information Per Serving

Serving Size: ¼ of Recipe • Calories 200 • Calories from Fat 25 • Total Fat 3 g
Saturated Fat 1 g • Cholesterol 75 mg • Sodium 200 mg • Dietary Fiber 1 g
Dietary Exchanges: 1 Fruit, 4 Very Lean Meat OR 1 Carbohydrate, 4 Very Lean Meat

---

Chicken Provençal

30 min. or less • *low-fat*

Prep Time: 20 minutes

1 tablespoon olive oil or vegetable oil
4 boneless, skinless chicken breast halves
1 large onion, sliced
1 cup cherry tomatoes, halved
1 (14-oz.) can artichoke hearts, drained, quartered
12 pitted extra-large ripe olives, halved

2 garlic cloves, minced
½ teaspoon dried rosemary leaves, crushed
¼ teaspoon fennel seed, crushed
½ cup purchased ready-to-serve fat-free chicken broth with ⅓ less sodium

1. Heat oil in large nonstick skillet over medium heat until hot. Add chicken; cook 4 minutes. Turn chicken; add onion. Cover; cook 3 minutes, stirring occasionally.
2. Add remaining ingredients. Cover; cook over medium-low heat for an additional 5 minutes, or until onion is crisp-tender, vegetables are hot, chicken is fork-tender and juices run clear. If desired, season to taste with salt and pepper.

Yield: 4 servings

Nutrition Information Per Serving

Serving Size: ¼ of Recipe • Calories 260 • Calories from Fat 80 • Total Fat 9 g
Saturated Fat 1.5 g • Cholesterol 75 mg • Sodium 460 mg • Dietary Fiber 5 g
Dietary Exchanges: 3 Vegetable, 3 Lean Meat

Recipe Fact

This chicken benefits from many of the characteristic flavors of the Provence region of France: olive oil, tomatoes, artichokes, olives, garlic and rosemary.

Kitchen Tip

Crushing the fennel seeds helps to release the flavor. If you don't have a mortar and pestle, chop the seeds a little bit with a chef's knife (carefully, so the seeds don't scatter all over the counter), or put them under a kitchen towel or piece of plastic wrap and crush them with a hammer, meat mallet or even the side of a 1- or 2-pound can.

Easy Chicken Parmigiana

Prep Time: 30 minutes

Recipe Fact

Parmigiana, an Italian term, describes food (usually veal, eggplant or chicken) cooked with Parmesan cheese.

About Penne Pasta

Penne is just one type of tubular-shaped pasta. Other "tunnel" noodles include mostaccioli, ziti and rigatoni. When the word **rigati** follows the noodle's name it means the surface is ridged rather than smooth.

About Ripe Olives

Ripe (black) olives range from very sweet, smooth, mild versions packed in brine to salty, chewy, wrinkled, oil-cured types. Pitted olives are easier to chop for cooking, though olives with pits usually have better texture.

6 oz. (2 cups) uncooked penne (medium pasta tubes)
¼ cup grated Parmesan cheese
¼ cup plain bread crumbs
4 boneless, skinless chicken breast halves
1 tablespoon oil
1 (14.5-oz.) can Italian-style tomatoes with olive oil, garlic and spices, undrained
1 small zucchini, cut into 1½-inch-long thin strips
2 tablespoons chopped ripe olives

1. Cook pasta to desired doneness as directed on package. Drain; cover to keep warm.

2. Meanwhile, in shallow bowl, combine cheese and bread crumbs; mix well. Coat chicken breast halves with cheese mixture. Heat oil in large skillet over medium-high heat until hot. Add chicken; cook 3 to 5 minutes on each side, or until browned.

3. Stir in tomatoes and zucchini. Bring to a boil. Reduce heat to low; cover and simmer 12 to 15 minutes, or until chicken is fork-tender and juices run clear, stirring and turning chicken occasionally. Serve chicken mixture with pasta. Sprinkle with olives.

Yield: 4 servings

Nutrition Information Per Serving

Serving Size: ¼ of Recipe • Calories 430 • Calories from Fat 110 • Total Fat 12 g
Saturated Fat 3 g • Cholesterol 80 mg • Sodium 800 mg • Dietary Fiber 3 g
Dietary Exchanges: 2 Starch, 2 Vegetable, 4 Lean Meat OR
2 Carbohydrate, 2 Vegetable, 4 Lean Meat

Easy Moo Goo Gai Pan

 low-fat

Prep Time: 40 minutes

4 cups cooked rice (cooked as
    directed on package)
4 boneless, skinless chicken
    breast halves, cut into thin
    strips
1 tablespoon cornstarch
1 tablespoon dry sherry
2 tablespoons soy sauce
1 cup chicken broth
4 teaspoons cornstarch
1 tablespoon oil
1 teaspoon grated gingerroot

2 garlic cloves, minced
8 oz. (2 cups) fresh snow pea
    pods, trimmed, cut
    diagonally in half
1 (8-oz.) can bamboo shoots,
    drained
1 (4.5-oz.) jar whole
    mushrooms, drained
3 green onions, cut into
    ½-inch pieces

1. In medium bowl, combine chicken, 1 tablespoon cornstarch, sherry and soy sauce; mix well. In small bowl,
combine broth and 4 teaspoons cornstarch; mix well.
2. Heat oil in large skillet or wok over medium-high heat
until hot. Add chicken mixture, gingerroot and garlic;
cook and stir 3 to 4 minutes, or until chicken is no longer
pink. Add pea pods, bamboo shoots and mushrooms; cook
and stir 3 to 4 minutes, or until vegetables are crisp-
tender.
3. Add broth mixture and green onions; cook until thickened and bubbly, stirring constantly. Serve over rice.

Yield: 4 servings

Nutrition Information Per Serving

Serving Size: ¼ of Recipe • Calories 450 • Calories from Fat 70 • Total Fat 8 g
Saturated Fat 2 g • Cholesterol 70 mg • Sodium 920 mg • Dietary Fiber 4 g
Dietary Exchanges: 3 Starch, 3 Vegetable, 3 Lean Meat OR
3 Carbohydrate, 3 Vegetable, 3 Lean Meat

Recipe Fact

Moo Goo Gai Pan is a
descriptive recipe name
that means chicken and
mushrooms in Chinese.

About Bamboo Shoots

Bamboo shoots, a com-
mon ingredient in Chi-
nese recipes, may be
available fresh in Asian
markets but are more typ-
ically sold in cans. The
ivory-colored vegetable
adds mild flavor and a bit
of texture to stir-fries.

Ingredient Substitution

Use canned Chinese straw
mushrooms or fresh shi-
itake mushrooms in place
of the canned button
mushrooms.

Easy Chicken Tetrazzini

Prep Time: 20 minutes

About Sherry

Sherry, a fortified wine that's a favorite drink of British society, hails from Spain, where it is known as **jeréz** or **xerés**. "Cooking sherry" has added salt and is not suitable for drinking, though it lends similar depth of flavor to cooked dishes.

Recipe Variation

Instead of serving the creamy chicken mixture over spaghetti, spoon it onto individual rounds of baked frozen puff pastry. Garnish each serving with chopped pimiento.

1 (7-oz.) pkg. uncooked spaghetti, broken into thirds
1 tablespoon margarine or butter
½ cup sliced green onions
1 (8-oz.) pkg. fresh mushrooms, sliced
3 tablespoons all-purpose flour
¼ teaspoon garlic powder
⅛ teaspoon pepper
1 cup chicken broth
½ cup skim milk
2 cups cubed cooked chicken
1 (2-oz.) jar sliced pimiento, drained
2 tablespoons dry sherry
¼ cup grated Parmesan cheese

1. In large saucepan, cook spaghetti to desired doneness as directed on package; drain and set aside in colander.

2. In same saucepan, melt margarine over medium-high heat. Add green onions and mushrooms; cook and stir until tender. In small bowl, combine flour, garlic powder, pepper, broth and milk; blend well. Add to onion mixture in saucepan. Cook until mixture boils and thickens, stirring constantly.

3. Add chicken, pimiento and sherry; cook until thoroughly heated, stirring occasionally. Stir in cheese. Add cooked spaghetti; toss gently. If desired, serve with additional grated Parmesan cheese and chopped fresh parsley.

Yield: 4 (1¼-cup) servings

Nutrition Information Per Serving
Serving Size: 1¼ Cups • Calories 430 • Calories from Fat 100 • Total Fat 11 g
Saturated Fat 3 g • Cholesterol 70 mg • Sodium 470 mg • Dietary Fiber 3 g
Dietary Exchanges: 3 Starch, 1 Vegetable, 3 Lean Meat OR
3 Carbohydrate, 1 Vegetable, 3 Lean Meat

Easy Chicken Tetrazzini

Rosemary Chicken with Grapes

Prep Time: 20 minutes

About Brown Rice

Brown rice is any rice that's still encased in its rough bran layer, which gives it a tan color. It has a slightly nut-like flavor from the endosperm. It takes 45 to 50 minutes to cook. Instant brown rice has been partially cooked and then dehydrated; it takes 5 to 15 minutes to cook, depending on the brand.

Menu Suggestion

Serve the chicken dish with steamed zucchini spears and whole wheat rolls.

2 cups cooked brown rice (cooked as directed on package)
¾ cup chicken broth
¼ cup white wine or white grape juice
1 tablespoon cornstarch
1 tablespoon oil

4 boneless, skinless chicken breast halves, cut into thin strips
¼ to ½ teaspoon dried rosemary leaves, crushed
1 cup sliced fresh mushrooms
¼ cup sliced green onions
1 cup seedless red grapes

1. In small bowl, combine broth, wine and cornstarch; blend well. Heat oil in large skillet over medium-high heat until hot. Add chicken and rosemary; cook and stir 4 to 5 minutes, or until chicken is no longer pink.
2. Add mushrooms and green onions; cook and stir 2 minutes. Add grapes and broth mixture. Cook and stir until mixture is thoroughly heated and sauce is thickened. Serve over rice.

Yield: 4 servings

Nutrition Information Per Serving

Serving Size: ¼ of Recipe • Calories 340 • Calories from Fat 70 • Total Fat 8 g
Saturated Fat 2 g • Cholesterol 75 mg • Sodium 210 mg • Dietary Fiber 2 g
Dietary Exchanges: 1 Starch, 1 Fruit, 4 Very Lean Meat, 1 Fat OR
2 Carbohydrate, 4 Very Lean Meat, 1 Fat

Fried Chicken

Prep Time: 50 minutes

⅓ cup all-purpose flour
1 teaspoon salt
¼ teaspoon pepper
¼ to ½ teaspoon poultry
   seasoning

3 to 3½ lb. cut-up frying
   chicken
1 cup oil or shortening

1. In plastic bag, combine flour, salt, pepper and poultry seasoning. Shake chicken, a few pieces at a time, in flour mixture to coat.

2. Heat oil in large skillet over medium heat; brown chicken on all sides.* Reduce heat to low; cover and simmer 30 minutes, or until chicken is fork-tender and juices run clear, removing cover last 10 minutes to crisp chicken.

Yield: 5 servings

*Tip: After browning, chicken can be placed in ungreased shallow baking pan and baked uncovered at 350°F. for about 45 minutes.

Nutrition Information Per Serving

Serving Size: ⅕ of Recipe • Calories 500 • Calories from Fat 330 • Total Fat 37 g
Saturated Fat 7 g • Cholesterol 110 mg • Sodium 530 mg • Dietary Fiber 0 g
Dietary Exchanges: ½ Starch, 5 Lean Meat, 4 Fat OR
½ Carbohydrate, 5 Lean Meat, 4 Fat

Recipe Fact

Old-fashioned fried chicken proves that simple techniques can yield absolutely mouthwatering results. The chicken is equally good hot from the pan or cold as a picnic treat.

Kitchen Tip

As the chicken fries, turn it gently with tongs to avoid piercing the skin. Transfer the cooked chicken to a plate lined with several layers of paper toweling to absorb excess grease.

Menu Suggestion

Serve the chicken with corn on the cob, homemade potato salad, dinner rolls, and sliced tomatoes and cucumbers drizzled with a garlicky vinaigrette. End the meal with watermelon wedges or slices of chocolate cake.

Light Chicken Chop Suey

• 30 min. or less • low-fat

Prep Time: 20 minutes

1 tablespoon cornstarch
½ teaspoon sugar
⅛ teaspoon garlic powder
½ cup chicken broth
1 to 2 tablespoons soy sauce
1 tablespoon dry sherry, if desired
1 teaspoon oil
4 boneless, skinless chicken breast halves, cut into ½-inch pieces

1 cup coarsely chopped red or green bell pepper
1 cup coarsely chopped celery
1 cup diagonally cut green onions (½-inch pieces)
1 (8-oz.) pkg. fresh bean sprouts

1. In small bowl, combine cornstarch, sugar, garlic powder, broth, soy sauce and sherry; blend well.

2. Heat oil in large nonstick skillet over medium-high heat until hot. Add chicken; cook and stir 3 to 4 minutes, or until chicken is no longer pink. Add bell pepper, celery and onions; cover and cook 3 to 5 minutes, or until vegetables are crisp-tender, stirring occasionally.

3. Stir in bean sprouts; cook about 1 minute, or until sprouts are thoroughly heated. Add cornstarch mixture to skillet; cook and stir until mixture thickens. If desired, serve with hot cooked rice.

Yield: 4 (1¼-cup) servings

Recipe Fact

Chop suey is not a Chinese dish but rather a Chinese-American creation. It's usually made with meat, chicken or shrimp, bean sprouts, bamboo shoots, water chestnuts, mushrooms and onions. This variation adds a touch of color with red or green pepper.

Kitchen Tip

Add the bean sprouts just before serving to keep them crisp and crunchy.

Nutrition Information Per Serving

Serving Size: 1¼ Cups • Calories 220 • Calories from Fat 60 • Total Fat 7 g
Saturated Fat 1 g • Cholesterol 70 mg • Sodium 730 mg • Dietary Fiber 3 g
Dietary Exchanges: 2 Vegetable, 3½ Very Lean Meat, 1 Fat

Light Chicken Chop Suey

Mediterranean Chicken and Bow Ties

Prep Time: 25 minutes

About Basil

Fresh basil, an annual herb, is the characteristic flavor in pesto and a natural partner for pasta as well as tomatoes and corn. Sweet basil is the type most often found in U.S. markets, though there are a number of different varieties—opal basil, lemon basil and Thai basil, to name a few—each with its own special flavor.

Menu Suggestion

For a simple focaccia-style accompaniment to the chicken, roll out purchased pizza dough and brush with olive oil. Sprinkle on a little salt, pepper and dried herbs (or minced fresh herbs) and bake at 450°F. until browned and cooked through, about 15 minutes. Accompany with a green salad and tiramisù or a fruit tart for dessert.

Pasta
4 quarts water
1 tablespoon chopped fresh basil or 1 teaspoon dried basil leaves
1 teaspoon chicken-flavor instant bouillon
8 oz. (3½ cups) uncooked bow tie pasta (farfalle)

Chicken
2 tablespoons olive oil or vegetable oil
4 boneless, skinless chicken breast halves, cut into ½-inch strips

1 garlic clove, minced
½ cup water
1 teaspoon cornstarch
½ cup diagonally cut green onions (½-inch pieces)
1 (2¼-oz.) can sliced pitted ripe olives, drained
¼ cup chopped fresh basil or 1 teaspoon dried basil leaves
½ teaspoon chicken-flavor instant bouillon
1 cup cherry tomato halves

1. Bring water, 1 tablespoon basil and 1 teaspoon bouillon to a boil. Add pasta; cook to desired doneness as directed on package. Drain; cover to keep warm.
2. Meanwhile, heat oil in large skillet over medium-high heat. Add chicken and garlic; cook and stir 6 to 9 minutes, or until chicken is no longer pink. In small bowl, combine ½ cup water and cornstarch; blend well. Stir into chicken.
3. Add green onions, olives, ¼ cup basil and ½ teaspoon bouillon; cook and stir 2 to 3 minutes, or until mixture is slightly thickened and glazed. Pour over pasta; add tomatoes and toss to coat. Garnish with fresh basil, if desired.

Yield: 4 servings

Nutrition Information Per Serving
Serving Size: ¼ of Recipe • Calories 440 • Calories from Fat 120 • Total Fat 13 g
Saturated Fat 2 g • Cholesterol 70 mg • Sodium 460 mg • Dietary Fiber 3 g
Dietary Exchanges: 3 Starch, 3½ Lean Meat OR 3 Carbohydrate, 3½ Lean Meat

Olive Chicken Parmesan

Prep Time: 40 minutes

¼ cup plain bread crumbs
¼ cup grated Parmesan cheese
½ teaspoon dried basil leaves
4 boneless, skinless chicken
    breast halves
1 egg, beaten
2 tablespoons olive oil or
    vegetable oil
1 (15-oz.) jar spaghetti sauce

½ cup water
¾ cup sliced green onions
½ cup sliced kalamata or ripe
    olives
8 oz. uncooked fettuccine
1 tablespoon olive oil or
    vegetable oil
1 oz. (¼ cup) shredded fresh
    Parmesan cheese

1. In shallow bowl, combine bread crumbs, ¼ cup grated Parmesan cheese and basil; mix well. Dip each chicken breast half in beaten egg; coat with bread crumb mixture.

2. Heat 2 tablespoons oil in large skillet over medium-high heat. Add chicken; brown well on both sides. Add spaghetti sauce and water. Cover; cook over low heat 15 to 20 minutes, or until chicken is fork-tender and juices run clear, stirring occasionally. Add green onions and olives; cook an additional 5 minutes.

3. Meanwhile, cook fettuccine to desired doneness as directed on package; drain. Toss with 1 tablespoon olive oil; place on serving platter. Spoon chicken and olive mixture over fettuccine; sprinkle with ¼ cup Parmesan cheese.

Yield: 4 servings

Nutrition Information Per Serving

Serving Size: ¼ of Recipe • Calories 690 • Calories from Fat 250 • Total Fat 28 g
Saturated Fat 6 g • Cholesterol 190 mg • Sodium 1050 mg • Dietary Fiber 6 g
Dietary Exchanges: 4 Starch, 1 Vegetable, 4 Lean Meat, 3 Fat OR
4 Carbohydrate, 1 Vegetable, 4 Lean Meat, 3 Fat

About Kalamata Olives

Purple-black kalamata olives are Greek in origin and gain their distinctive flavor from a wine vinegar brine.

Make It Special

Surround the noodles on the platter with fresh basil leaves. Reserve a few whole olives and use them, along with additional fresh basil leaves, to garnish the top.

Piccata Chicken

Prep Time: 30 minutes

Recipe Fact

Piccata is a famous Italian dish, usually made with veal, in which thin slices of meat are seasoned, floured, quickly cooked and served with a sauce of pan drippings, lemon juice and parsley.

Menu Suggestion

Serve the chicken with a crisp white wine, brown rice, steamed broccoli and sliced tomatoes. For dessert, try pound cake with fresh berries.

4 boneless, skinless chicken breast halves
¼ cup all-purpose flour
¼ teaspoon salt
¼ teaspoon white pepper
2 tablespoons oil
½ cup chicken broth

2 teaspoons Worcestershire sauce
¼ teaspoon dried marjoram leaves
2 tablespoons fresh lemon juice
¼ cup chopped fresh parsley

1. Place 1 chicken breast half between 2 pieces of plastic wrap or waxed paper. Working from center, gently pound chicken with flat side of meat mallet or rolling pin until about ¼ inch thick; remove wrap. Repeat with remaining chicken breast halves.

2. In shallow bowl, combine flour, salt and pepper. Coat chicken breast halves with flour mixture. Heat oil in large skillet over medium-high heat until hot. Add chicken; cook 3 to 5 minutes on each side, or until golden brown, fork-tender and juices run clear.

3. Remove chicken from skillet; cover to keep warm. Add broth, Worcestershire sauce and marjoram to skillet; cook and stir 1 to 2 minutes. Stir in lemon juice and parsley. Serve over chicken.

Yield: 4 servings

Nutrition Information Per Serving

Serving Size: ¼ of Recipe • Calories 230 • Calories from Fat 90 • Total Fat 10 g
Saturated Fat 2 g • Cholesterol 75 mg • Sodium 320 mg • Dietary Fiber 0 g
Dietary Exchanges: ½ Starch, 3½ Lean Meat OR ½ Carbohydrate, 3½ Lean Meat

---

Piccata Chicken

Pineapple Chicken and Rice

Prep Time: 50 minutes

About Bell Peppers

Bell peppers come in many colors, including green, red, yellow, orange, purple and brown. Red peppers are actually just green peppers that have been allowed to ripen on the plant. Peppers are an excellent source of vitamin C and also provide vitamin A.

Make It Special

Sprinkle servings with toasted coconut and chopped toasted macadamia nuts.

2 tablespoons oil
4 bone-in chicken breast halves, skin removed, if desired
1 (14½-oz.) can ready-to-serve chicken broth
½ cup purchased sweet-and-sour sauce
1 (8-oz.) can pineapple tidbits in unsweetened juice, drained, reserving liquid

1 cup uncooked regular long-grain white rice
½ cup chopped red bell pepper
½ cup chopped green bell pepper
½ cup sliced green onions

1. Heat oil in large skillet over medium-high heat until hot. Add chicken; cook 2 to 3 minutes on each side, or until browned. Remove chicken from skillet.

2. Add chicken broth, sweet-and-sour sauce, pineapple liquid and rice to skillet; blend well. Bring to a boil. Add chicken breast halves, meaty side down. Reduce heat to low; cover and simmer 25 to 30 minutes, or until most of the liquid is absorbed, chicken is fork-tender and juices run clear.

3. Remove chicken from skillet; cover to keep warm. Add bell peppers, green onions and pineapple tidbits to rice mixture. Cook an additional 5 minutes, or until peppers are crisp-tender. Spoon rice mixture onto platter; top with chicken.

Yield: 4 servings

Pineapple Chicken and Rice

Nutrition Information Per Serving
Serving Size: ¼ of Recipe • Calories 510 • Calories from Fat 140 • Total Fat 15 g
Saturated Fat 3 g • Cholesterol 80 mg • Sodium 500 mg • Dietary Fiber 2 g
Dietary Exchanges: 3 Starch, 1 Fruit, 4 Lean Meat OR 4 Carbohydrate, 4 Lean Meat

Salsa Chicken Cacciatore

Prep Time: 55 minutes

Recipe Fact

Chicken cacciatore means "hunter's-style chicken" and typically consists of chicken browned in oil, then simmered with tomatoes and often mushrooms.

Ingredient Substitution

For a more traditional cacciatore, use 1 cup sliced fresh mushrooms in place of the corn.

2 tablespoons oil
3 to 3½ lb. cut-up frying chicken, skin removed
¼ cup all-purpose flour
1 (14.5-oz.) can salsa-style chunky tomatoes, undrained

1 teaspoon chili powder
½ teaspoon dried oregano leaves
1 cup frozen whole kernel corn

1. Heat oil in large skillet over medium-high heat until hot. Coat chicken pieces with flour; add to skillet. Cook 4 to 5 minutes on each side, or until browned; drain. Stir in tomatoes, chili powder and oregano. Bring to a boil. Reduce heat to low; cover and simmer 30 minutes.

2. Stir in corn; cover and cook an additional 10 to 15 minutes, or until chicken is fork-tender and juices run clear, stirring occasionally.

Yield: 5 servings

Nutrition Information Per Serving

Serving Size: ⅕ of Recipe • Calories 320 • Calories from Fat 120 • Total Fat 13 g
Saturated Fat 3 g • Cholesterol 90 mg • Sodium 240 mg • Dietary Fiber 2 g
Dietary Exchanges: 1 Starch, 1 Vegetable, 4 Lean Meat OR
1 Carbohydrate, 1 Vegetable, 4 Lean Meat

Skillet Arroz con Pollo

Prep Time: 40 minutes

2 teaspoons olive oil
4 chicken legs, skin removed
4 chicken thighs, skin removed
1 (14½-oz.) can ready-to-serve
    chicken broth
1 cup uncooked converted or
    regular long-grain white
    rice

½ cup sliced green onions
½ cup chopped red or green
    bell pepper
¼ teaspoon turmeric or saffron
⅛ teaspoon garlic powder
⅛ to ¼ teaspoon ground red
    pepper (cayenne)

1. Heat oil in large nonstick skillet over medium-high heat until hot. Add chicken; cook until browned on all sides. Move chicken to side of skillet. Add remaining ingredients; blend well. Place chicken in rice mixture. Bring to a boil. Reduce heat to low; cover and simmer 15 minutes, stirring occasionally.

2. Turn chicken; cover and simmer an additional 5 to 10 minutes, or until chicken is fork-tender and juices run clear.

Yield: 4 servings

Nutrition Information Per Serving

Serving Size: ¼ of Recipe • Calories 390 • Calories from Fat 100 • Total Fat 11 g
Saturated Fat 3 g • Cholesterol 90 mg • Sodium 420 mg • Dietary Fiber 1 g
Dietary Exchanges: 2 Starch, 2 Vegetable, 3 Lean Meat, ½ Fat OR
2 Carbohydrate, 2 Vegetable, 3 Lean Meat, ½ Fat

Recipe Fact

Arroz con pollo is Spanish for "rice with chicken."

About Saffron

Saffron, the world's most expensive spice, is the aromatic stamen (threads in the center of the flower) of a certain crocus. A single pound of saffron requires the stamens from 80,000 crocuses. Saffron is sold in minute quantities, often in little clear glass or plastic vials. It's best to buy it in whole threads rather than ground so you can be sure of what you're getting (ground mixtures may be adulterated with inexpensive substances of a similar color). Because a little goes a long way, saffron is affordable for occasional use. Its flavor is distinctive. Turmeric, an often-suggested inexpensive substitute, adds similar color but cannot match the flavor of saffron.

Saucy Chicken and Peaches

Prep Time: 20 minutes

1 teaspoon oil
4 boneless, skinless chicken breast halves
1 (16-oz.) can sliced peaches in light syrup, undrained
1 tablespoon cornstarch

2 tablespoons brown sugar
1 tablespoon cider vinegar
1 tablespoon soy sauce
½ to 1 teaspoon dried basil leaves

1. Heat oil in large nonstick skillet over medium heat until hot. Add chicken; cook 4 to 5 minutes, or until lightly browned. Turn chicken; cover and cook an additional 4 to 5 minutes, or until chicken is fork-tender and juices run clear. Remove from skillet; cover to keep warm.
2. Meanwhile, drain peach syrup into glass measuring cup; add water to make 1 cup liquid. Stir in cornstarch, brown sugar, vinegar, soy sauce and basil.
3. Pour liquid into hot skillet; cook and stir until thickened and bubbly. Gently stir in peach slices and chicken. If desired, serve with hot cooked rice.

Yield: 4 servings

Nutrition Information Per Serving

Serving Size: ¼ of Recipe • Calories 250 • Calories from Fat 35 • Total Fat 4 g
Saturated Fat 1 g • Cholesterol 75 mg • Sodium 330 mg • Dietary Fiber 1 g
Dietary Exchanges: 2 Fruit, 4 Very Lean Meat OR
2 Carbohydrate, 4 Very Lean Meat

Ingredient Substitution

Substitute canned apricots for the peaches.

Ingredient Substitution

Substitute orange juice for the peach syrup and 2 or 3 sliced fresh peaches or nectarines for the canned fruit.

Menu Suggestion

Serve the chicken with hot cooked rice accompanied by coleslaw and steamed green beans. End the meal with spice cake and coffee.

Saucy Chicken and Peaches

Tangy Sesame Chicken

Prep Time: 1 hour

About Sesame Oil

Sesame oil, a key flavor ingredient in Asian cooking, is extremely pungent. A tiny amount flavors an entire dish. It's available in light and dark forms (the darker is stronger in flavor) as well as regular or hot (with chile peppers added).

Kitchen Tip

For chicken with a crisp, nicely browned outside and tender, moist interior, be sure not to crowd the pan during frying; be patient and work in batches, or use a very large pan that will fit all the food comfortably.

4 oz. uncooked Chinese lo mein noodles
¼ cup cornstarch
2 tablespoons all-purpose flour
1 teaspoon sugar
¼ teaspoon baking soda
¼ cup water
¼ teaspoon sesame oil
2 boneless, skinless chicken breast halves, cut into ½-inch strips

Oil for frying
1 medium green bell pepper, cut into strips
1 teaspoon sesame seed
1 cup purchased sweet-and-sour sauce
1 tablespoon sugar
2 tablespoons rice vinegar
½ teaspoon sesame oil

1. Cook noodles as directed on package. Drain; cover to keep warm.
2. In medium bowl, combine cornstarch, flour, 1 teaspoon sugar and baking soda. Stir in water and ¼ teaspoon sesame oil. Add chicken; mix well to combine.*
3. In deep-fryer, heavy saucepan or wok, heat 2 to 3 inches of oil to 375° F. Shaking off excess batter, fry chicken strips a few at a time for 3 to 5 minutes, or until light golden brown and no longer pink in center. Drain on paper towels. (Reserve 1 tablespoon oil from deep frying.)
4. Heat reserved 1 tablespoon oil in large skillet or wok over medium-high heat until hot. Add bell pepper and sesame seed; cook and stir 2 to 3 minutes, or until pepper is crisp-tender and seed is golden brown.
5. Add sweet-and-sour sauce, 1 tablespoon sugar, vinegar and ½ teaspoon sesame oil; mix well. Add chicken strips; cook 1 to 2 minutes, stirring constantly, or until thoroughly heated. Serve over noodles.

Yield: 3 servings

*Tip: If coating mixture is too thick, add additional water 1 teaspoon at a time to thin.

Tangy Sesame Chicken

Subgum Chicken Stir-Fry

Recipe Fact

Subgum is a Chinese term that means "with vegetables."

About Oyster Sauce

Oyster sauce, a thick brown mixture available in supermarkets and Asian groceries, contains primarily water, sugar, oyster extractives and cornstarch. It serves as a flavor enhancer and sauce thickener.

About Bok Choy

Bok choy, a member of the cabbage family, has thick white stalks, dark green leaves and a mild flavor. It adds good texture and color to stir-fry dishes. It's also good on its own, chopped and steamed as a side dish.

Prep Time: 20 minutes

4 cups cooked rice (cooked as directed on package)
1 cup chicken broth
2 tablespoons cornstarch
3 tablespoons oyster sauce
2 teaspoons soy sauce
1 tablespoon oil
¼ cup chopped onion
1 garlic clove, minced
4 boneless, skinless chicken breast halves, cut into 1-inch pieces
1 cup thinly sliced bok choy
1 cup fresh bean sprouts
1 medium green bell pepper, cut into ¼-inch strips
1 (8-oz.) can sliced bamboo shoots, drained

1. In small bowl, combine chicken broth, cornstarch, oyster sauce and soy sauce.

2. Heat oil in large skillet or wok over medium-high heat until hot. Add onion, garlic and chicken; cook and stir 3 to 4 minutes, or until chicken is no longer pink. Add bok choy, bean sprouts, bell pepper and bamboo shoots; cook and stir 3 to 4 minutes, or until vegetables are crisp-tender. Gradually add cornstarch mixture; cook until thickened and bubbly, stirring constantly. Serve over rice.

Yield: 4 servings

Nutrition Information Per Serving

Serving Size: ¼ of Recipe • Calories 430 • Calories from Fat 60 • Total Fat 7 g
Saturated Fat 2 g • Cholesterol 70 mg • Sodium 1040 mg • Dietary Fiber 3 g
Dietary Exchanges: 3 Starch, 2 Vegetable, 2½ Lean Meat OR
3 Carbohydrate, 2 Vegetable, 2½ Lean Meat

Sage and Rosemary Chicken Strips

Prep Time: 20 minutes

⅓ cup all-purpose flour
½ teaspoon onion powder
¼ teaspoon salt
¼ teaspoon dried rosemary
    leaves, crushed

⅛ teaspoon ground sage
4 boneless, skinless chicken
    breast halves, cut into long,
    thin strips
1 tablespoon oil

1. In shallow bowl, combine flour, onion powder, salt, rosemary and sage; mix well. Generously coat chicken pieces with flour mixture.

2. Heat oil in large skillet over medium-high heat until hot. Add chicken; reduce heat to medium. Cook and stir 8 to 10 minutes, or until lightly browned on all sides and no longer pink.

Yield: 4 servings

Nutrition Information Per Serving

Serving Size: ¼ of Recipe • Calories 210 • Calories from Fat 60 • Total Fat 7 g
Saturated Fat 1 g • Cholesterol 75 mg • Sodium 200 mg • Dietary Fiber 0 g
Dietary Exchanges: ½ Starch, 4 Very Lean Meat, ½ Fat OR
½ Carbohydrate, 4 Very Lean Meat, ½ Fat

Kitchen Tip

Fry the chicken immediately after flouring it so the coating doesn't become soggy.

Recipe Variation

Instead of flavoring the flour with rosemary and sage, substitute ¼ teaspoon ground cumin and ¼ teaspoon chili powder.

Menu Suggestion

Accompany with spinach salad, corn on the cob and fresh fruit cup.

Baked

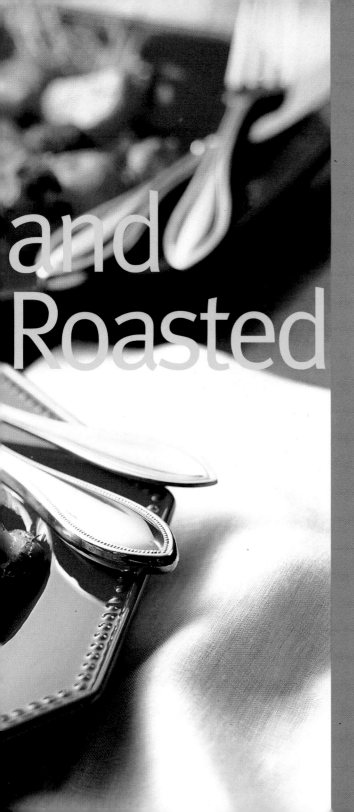

and Roasted Entrees

Baking and roasting chicken in the oven hold timeless appeal, and for good reason. While initial preparations may involve chopping and mixing, the bird generally requires little or no attention during cooking time (except perhaps occasional basting); the cook can tend to other kitchen chores or even relax while the appealing and unmistakable aroma of roasting chicken fills the house.

Baked and Roasted Entrees

Previous page: Roasted Chicken and Vegetables Provençal page 181

Roasted Chicken and Vegetables Provençal

Prep Time: 30 minutes
(Ready in 1 hour 35 minutes)

8 small new red potatoes, quartered
1 small yellow squash, cut into 1-inch pieces
1 small zucchini, cut into 1-inch pieces
1 medium red bell pepper, cut into 1-inch pieces
1 medium red onion, cut into eighths
1 (8-oz.) pkg. fresh mushrooms
¼ cup olive oil
2 teaspoons dried basil leaves
2 teaspoons dried thyme leaves
½ teaspoon salt
½ teaspoon coarsely ground black pepper
3 garlic cloves, minced
3 to 3½ lb. cut-up frying chicken, skin removed

1. Heat oven to 375°F. In ungreased 13 × 9-inch (3-quart) baking dish, combine potatoes, squash, zucchini, bell pepper, onion and mushrooms.

2. In small bowl, combine oil, basil, thyme, salt, pepper and garlic; mix well. Brush half of oil mixture on vegetables. Place chicken pieces, meaty side up, over vegetables. Brush chicken with remaining oil mixture.

3. Bake at 375°F. for 45 minutes. Baste with pan juices; bake an additional 15 to 20 minutes, or until chicken is fork-tender, its juices run clear and vegetables are tender. Baste with pan juices before serving.

Yield: 4 servings

Nutrition Information Per Serving
Serving Size: ¼ of Recipe • Calories 550 • Calories from Fat 220 • Total Fat 24 g
Saturated Fat 5 g • Cholesterol 115 mg • Sodium 390 mg • Dietary Fiber 6 g
Dietary Exchanges: 2 Starch, 2 Vegetable, 4½ Lean Meat, 2 Fat OR
2 Carbohydrate, 2 Vegetable, 4½ Lean Meat, 2 Fat

About Red Pepper

A red bell pepper is just a green bell pepper that has been allowed to ripen on the vine, becoming sweet in the process. Because the ripe pepper is more perishable, it is almost always more expensive than the green.

About Mushrooms

When preparing fresh mushrooms, don't soak them in water—they'll get too mushy. Instead, brush off any loose dirt, then wipe them with a damp paper towel.

Menu Suggestion

Serve this country-style roasted chicken dinner with fresh tomato slices drizzled with balsamic vinegar and sprinkled with minced fresh herbs and garlic bread.

Caramelized Garlic Chicken

30 min. or less • low-fat • editor's choice

Make It Special

Cut each breast into thin slices and arrange in a fan formation on a bed of wild rice. Garnish with sprigs of parsley.

Menu Suggestion

Accompany the chicken with fettuccine and steamed broccoli.

Prep Time: 25 minutes

4 garlic cloves, minced
2 teaspoons olive oil
4 teaspoons brown sugar

4 boneless, skinless chicken
   breast halves

1. Heat oven to 500°F. Line shallow roasting pan with foil; spray foil with nonstick cooking spray.
2. In small nonstick skillet, combine garlic and oil; cook and stir over medium-low heat for 1 to 2 minutes, or until garlic begins to soften. Remove from heat. Stir in brown sugar; mix well.
3. Place chicken breast halves in sprayed foil-lined pan; spread garlic mixture evenly over chicken.
4. Bake at 500°F. for 10 to 15 minutes, or until chicken is fork-tender and juices run clear.

Yield: 4 servings

Nutrition Information Per Serving

Serving Size: ¼ of Recipe • Calories 170 • Calories from Fat 45 • Total Fat 5 g
Saturated Fat 1 g • Cholesterol 75 mg • Sodium 65 mg • Dietary Fiber 0 g
Dietary Exchanges: ½ Fruit, 4 Very Lean Meat OR
½ Carbohydrate, 4 Very Lean Meat

Caramelized Garlic Chicken

Baked Chicken Peanut Kabobs

Recipe Fact

This flavor-packed dish takes its inspiration from the Indonesian specialty called satay—skewers of marinated meat, poultry or fish usually served with peanut sauce.

Make-Ahead Tip

You can cut up the chicken, mushrooms and green onions several hours in advance; wrap them separately in plastic and refrigerate until cooking time.

Menu Suggestion

Serve the kabobs with steamed green beans, rice pilaf and sliced tomatoes sprinkled with minced chives.

Prep Time: 35 minutes

4 boneless, skinless chicken breast halves, cut into 1-inch pieces
12 whole fresh mushrooms
6 green onions, cut into 2-inch pieces

½ cup purchased teriyaki sauce
1 tablespoon oil
¼ cup creamy peanut butter
¼ teaspoon hot pepper sauce

1. Heat oven to 450°F. Spray broiler pan with nonstick cooking spray. Alternately thread chicken, mushrooms and green onions on six 8- to 12-inch metal skewers. Place on sprayed broiler pan.
2. In small bowl, combine 2 tablespoons of the teriyaki sauce and oil; mix well. Brush on kabobs.
3. Bake at 450°F. for 18 to 20 minutes, or until chicken is no longer pink, turning once and brushing with teriyaki and oil mixture. Discard any remaining teriyaki and oil mixture.
4. To prepare sauce, in medium bowl, combine remaining teriyaki sauce, peanut butter and hot pepper sauce; mix well. Using a clean brush, brush sauce on kabobs before serving. Serve with remaining sauce.

Yield: 6 servings

Nutrition Information Per Serving

Serving Size: ⅙ of Recipe • Calories 200 • Calories from Fat 70 • Total Fat 8 g
Saturated Fat 2 g • Cholesterol 50 mg • Sodium 850 mg • Dietary Fiber 1 g
Dietary Exchanges: ½ Fruit, 2 Lean Meat OR ½ Carbohydrate, 2 Lean Meat

---

Baked Chicken Peanut Kabobs

Easy Baked Chicken and Potato Dinner

Prep Time: 15 minutes
(Ready in 50 minutes)

4 bone-in chicken breast halves, skin removed

4 medium russet or Idaho baking potatoes, unpeeled, cut into 1-inch cubes

1 medium red or green bell pepper, cut into 1 × ½-inch pieces

1 medium onion, cut into 8 wedges

2 tablespoons margarine or butter, melted

¼ cup grated Parmesan cheese

1 teaspoon garlic powder

1 teaspoon paprika

1. Heat oven to 400°F. Spray 15 × 10 × 1-inch baking pan with nonstick cooking spray. Place 1 chicken breast half in each corner of sprayed pan. Place potatoes, bell pepper and onion in center of pan. Pour melted margarine over chicken and vegetables; sprinkle evenly with cheese, garlic powder and paprika.

2. Bake at 400°F. for 30 to 35 minutes, or until chicken is fork-tender and juices run clear, stirring vegetables once halfway through cooking.

Yield: 4 servings

Nutrition Information Per Serving

Serving Size: ¼ of Recipe • Calories 370 • Calories from Fat 100 • Total Fat 11 g
Saturated Fat 3 g • Cholesterol 80 mg • Sodium 260 mg • Dietary Fiber 4 g
Dietary Exchanges: 2 Starch, 1 Vegetable, 3 Lean Meat, ½ Fat OR
2 Carbohydrate, 1 Vegetable, 3 Lean Meat, ½ Fat

Chicken Tetrazzini Casserole

Prep Time: 20 minutes
(Ready in 55 minutes)

7 oz. uncooked spaghetti
¼ cup margarine or butter
8 oz. fresh mushrooms, sliced
3 tablespoons all-purpose flour
2 cups chicken broth
¾ cup half-and-half
3 tablespoons dry sherry, if desired
1 tablespoon chopped fresh parsley

½ teaspoon salt
⅛ teaspoon nutmeg
Dash pepper
3 cups cubed cooked chicken
¾ cup grated Parmesan cheese
1 to 2 teaspoons chopped fresh parsley, if desired

1. Heat oven to 350°F. Cook spaghetti to desired doneness as directed on package. Drain; rinse with hot water. Cover to keep warm.

2. Meanwhile, in Dutch oven or large saucepan, melt margarine over medium heat. Add mushrooms; cook until tender, stirring occasionally. Stir in flour; cook and stir 1 minute, or until smooth and bubbly. Gradually stir in chicken broth. Cook and stir over medium heat until slightly thickened and bubbly. Remove from heat.

3. Add half-and-half, sherry, 1 tablespoon parsley, salt, nutmeg and pepper; mix well. Add chicken and cooked spaghetti; toss to combine. Spoon into ungreased 13 × 9-inch (3-quart) baking dish; sprinkle with cheese.

4. Bake at 350°F. for 30 to 35 minutes, or until thoroughly heated. Just before serving, sprinkle with parsley.

Yield: 10 servings

Nutrition Information Per Serving

Serving Size: ¹⁄₁₀ of Recipe • Calories 280 • Calories from Fat 120 • Total Fat 13 g
Saturated Fat 5 g • Cholesterol 50 mg • Sodium 500 mg • Dietary Fiber 1 g
Dietary Exchanges: 1 Starch, 1 Vegetable, 2 Lean Meat, 1½ Fat OR
1 Carbohydrate, 1 Vegetable, 2 Lean Meat, 1½ Fat

Recipe Fact

White sauce, the basis for a host of dishes, has a classic formula of 2 tablespoons of butter (or other fat) and 2 tablespoons of flour per cup of milk.

Make-Ahead Tip

Prepare both the white rice and the wild rice ahead of time (or use leftovers from a previous meal) and store them in the refrigerator or the freezer until you're ready to complete the casserole.

Chicken, Artichoke and Rice Casserole

Prep Time: 30 minutes
(Ready in 2 hours 30 minutes)

White Sauce*
6 tablespoons margarine or butter
6 tablespoons all-purpose flour
½ teaspoon salt
¼ teaspoon pepper
1½ cups chicken broth
1 cup milk

Casserole
1 tablespoon margarine or butter
2 cups julienne-cut (2 × ¼ × ¼-inch) carrots
½ cup chopped green bell pepper

⅓ cup chopped green onions
½ cup milk
¼ cup dry sherry
2½ cups cubed cooked chicken
2 slices bacon, cooked until crisp, crumbled
8 oz. (2 cups) shredded mozzarella cheese
1½ cups cooked white rice
1½ cups cooked wild rice
1 to 2 (14-oz.) cans artichoke hearts, drained, quartered
¼ cup grated Parmesan cheese
1 to 2 teaspoons dried parsley flakes

1. In medium saucepan, melt 6 tablespoons margarine over medium heat. Stir in flour, salt and pepper. Cook until mixture is smooth and bubbly, stirring constantly. Gradually stir in chicken broth and 1 cup milk. Cook until mixture boils and thickens, stirring constantly.

2. Heat oven to 350°F. Grease 13 × 9-inch (3-quart) baking dish. In large skillet, melt 1 tablespoon margarine over medium-high heat. Add carrots, bell pepper and green onions; cook and stir until crisp-tender. Stir in white sauce, ½ cup milk, sherry, chicken, bacon and mozzarella cheese; blend well. Remove from heat.

3. Combine white and wild rice; spread evenly over bottom of greased baking dish. Arrange artichokes over rice. Spoon chicken mixture evenly over artichokes.** Sprinkle with Parmesan cheese and parsley flakes; cover tightly with foil.

4. Bake at 350°F. for 40 minutes. Uncover; bake an additional 15 to 20 minutes, or until casserole is thoroughly heated.

Yield: 12 servings

*Tip: Two (10¾-oz.) cans condensed cream of chicken soup (undiluted) can be substituted for the White Sauce.

**Recipe can be prepared to this point, covered and refrigerated up to 24 hours. Sprinkle casserole with Parmesan cheese and parsley flakes; cover tightly with foil. Bake at 350°F. for 60 minutes. Uncover; bake an additional 15 to 20 minutes, or until casserole is thoroughly heated.

Nutrition Information Per Serving

Serving Size: ¹⁄₁₂ of Recipe • Calories 300 • Calories from Fat 130 • Total Fat 14 g
Saturated Fat 5 g • Cholesterol 40 mg • Sodium 510 mg • Dietary Fiber 4 g
Dietary Exchanges: 1½ Starch, 2 Lean Meat, 1½ Fat OR
1½ Carbohydrate, 2 Lean Meat, 1½ Fat

Chicken, Artichoke and Rice Casserole

Chicken Breasts with Wild Rice

Prep Time: 15 minutes
(Ready in 2 hours 30 minutes)

1 cup uncooked wild rice
½ cup chopped onion
3 cups water
½ cup sour cream
1 (10¾-oz.) can condensed cream of chicken soup
½ teaspoon dried thyme leaves
½ teaspoon dried marjoram leaves
½ teaspoon salt
¼ teaspoon pepper
1 (9-oz.) pkg. frozen asparagus cuts in a pouch, thawed, drained
6 bone-in chicken breast halves, skin removed
½ teaspoon seasoned salt

1. Heat oven to 350°F. In medium saucepan, combine wild rice, onion and water. Bring to a boil. Reduce heat to low; cover and simmer 45 to 55 minutes, or until rice is tender and water is absorbed. DO NOT DRAIN.

2. Add sour cream, soup, thyme, marjoram, salt and pepper to rice mixture in saucepan; blend well. Spread mixture evenly in ungreased 13 × 9-inch (3-quart) baking dish. Top with asparagus. Place chicken breast halves over asparagus, meaty side up; sprinkle with seasoned salt.

3. Bake at 350°F. for 1 to 1¼ hours, or until chicken is fork-tender and juices run clear.

Yield: 6 servings

Nutrition Information Per Serving

Serving Size: ⅙ of Recipe • Calories 350 • Calories from Fat 100 • Total Fat 11 g
Saturated Fat 4 g • Cholesterol 85 mg • Sodium 820 mg • Dietary Fiber 3 g
Dietary Exchanges: 1½ Starch, 1 Vegetable, 4 Lean Meat OR
1½ Carbohydrate, 1 Vegetable, 4 Lean Meat

Chicken Spinach Pizza

Prep Time: 30 minutes

- 30 min. or less
- low-fat
- editor's choice

1 (10-oz.) can refrigerated pizza crust

2 cups frozen cut leaf spinach, cooked, well drained

1½ cups chopped cooked chicken

3 to 4 thinly sliced Italian plum tomatoes

¼ teaspoon garlic powder

¼ teaspoon dried marjoram leaves

6 oz. (1½ cups) shredded Swiss cheese

1. Heat oven to 400°F. Grease 12-inch pizza pan. Unroll dough; place in greased pan. Starting at center, press out with hands. Bake at 400°F. for 7 to 9 minutes.

2. Top partially baked crust with remaining ingredients. Bake an additional 12 to 15 minutes, or until cheese is melted and crust is golden brown.

Yield: 8 servings

Nutrition Information Per Serving

Serving Size: ⅛ of Recipe • Calories 240 • Calories from Fat 80 • Total Fat 9 g
Saturated Fat 5 g • Cholesterol 45 mg • Sodium 320 mg • Dietary Fiber 2 g
Dietary Exchanges: 1 Starch, 1 Vegetable, 2 Medium-Fat Meat OR
1 Carbohydrate, 1 Vegetable, 2 Medium-Fat Meat

Ingredient Substitution

Try 6 ounces of fresh mozzarella in place of the Swiss cheese.

Make It Special

Instead of simply scattering the toppings over the crust, arrange them artfully. Place the tomato slices in a ring around the edge of the pie and spread the spinach in the center.

Chicken Breasts with Wild Rice

Coq au Vin

Recipe Fact

Coq au vin, a French peasant classic, is a recipe designed to tenderize a tough chicken through slow simmering in red wine.

Menu Suggestion

Serve this moist, tender chicken with hearty red wine, rice, tossed salad and a loaf of French bread.

8 slices bacon, cut into ½-inch pieces

3 to 3½ lb. cut-up frying chicken, skin removed, if desired

1½ cups frozen small whole onions

1 (4.5-oz.) jar whole mushrooms, drained

2 tablespoons chopped fresh parsley

½ teaspoon dried thyme leaves

2 garlic cloves, minced

¼ cup all-purpose flour

1½ cups dry red wine

1 to 2 teaspoons chopped fresh parsley, if desired

1. Heat oven to 400°F. Cook bacon in large skillet or Dutch oven over medium heat until crisp. Remove bacon from skillet; reserve drippings. Brown chicken in hot bacon drippings, turning to brown all sides; drain. Place chicken in 2½- to 3-quart casserole; sprinkle with bacon.

2. In same skillet, combine onions, mushrooms, 2 tablespoons parsley, thyme and garlic. Cook over medium heat until thoroughly heated, stirring occasionally. Stir in flour; gradually stir in wine. Cook until mixture boils and thickens, stirring constantly. Pour over chicken and bacon in casserole; cover tightly.

3. Bake at 400°F. for 40 to 50 minutes, or until chicken is fork-tender and juices run clear. Sprinkle with parsley.

Yield: 6 servings

Nutrition Information Per Serving

Serving Size: ⅙ of Recipe • Calories 290 • Calories from Fat 100 • Total Fat 11 g
Saturated Fat 3 g • Cholesterol 85 mg • Sodium 310 mg • Dietary Fiber 1 g
Dietary Exchanges: ½ Starch, 1 Vegetable, 4 Lean Meat OR
½ Carbohydrate, 1 Vegetable, 4 Lean Meat

Garlic Roasted Chicken

Prep Time: 10 minutes
(Ready in 1 hour 5 minutes)

3 to 3½ lb. cut-up frying
   chicken, skin removed
3 tablespoons margarine or
   butter, melted
1 tablespoon dried parsley
   flakes

2 tablespoons soy sauce
1 teaspoon cornstarch
½ teaspoon grated gingerroot
4 to 6 garlic cloves, minced

1. Heat oven to 350°F. Arrange chicken pieces in ungreased 12 × 8-inch (2-quart) baking dish. In small bowl, combine remaining ingredients; blend well. Brush chicken with soy mixture.
2. Bake at 350°F. for 45 to 55 minutes, or until chicken is fork-tender and juices run clear, basting with drippings halfway through cooking.

Yield: 4 servings

Nutrition Information Per Serving
Serving Size: ¼ of Recipe • Calories 330 • Calories from Fat 160 • Total Fat 18 g
Saturated Fat 4 g • Cholesterol 115 mg • Sodium 730 mg • Dietary Fiber 0 g
Dietary Exchanges: 5½ Lean Meat, ½ Fat

About Garlic

Garlic's flavor is most potent when it's added to a dish raw. Its flavor is tamed by cooking—the longer you cook it, the more mellow it becomes. The way you cut up garlic affects its strength, too. The more you chop or mince it, the stronger its flavor. For the most delicate flavor, cook with whole cloves—unpeeled—and remove them before serving.

About Fresh Ginger

Fresh ginger, a knobby root, adds pungent flavor to dishes and is an especially good complement to garlic. At cooking time, peel off the thin brown skin with a sharp paring knife or vegetable peeler, then grate the stringy yellow flesh with a fine-holed grater.

Crescent Chicken Newburg

Recipe Fact

Newburg is a rich, elegant dish usually made with shrimp, butter, cream and sherry. This chicken-studded version is a meal in a dish, with protein, vegetables and dinner rolls all in one.

Healthy Hint

The dish is slightly less rich-tasting made with 2 percent milk instead of half-and-half, but you save 50 calories and 6 grams of fat per serving.

Prep Time: 25 minutes
(Ready in 55 minutes)

2 tablespoons margarine or butter
6 boneless, skinless chicken breast halves, cut into ½-inch pieces
¼ cup all-purpose flour
¼ to ½ teaspoon salt
¼ teaspoon white pepper
1½ cups half-and-half
3 tablespoons dry sherry
1 (16-oz.) pkg. frozen broccoli, carrots and water chestnuts, cooked, drained

2 tablespoons grated Parmesan cheese
1 (8-oz.) can refrigerated crescent dinner rolls
1 tablespoon margarine or butter, melted
1 tablespoon grated Parmesan cheese
¼ teaspoon paprika

1. Heat oven to 350°F. In large skillet, melt 2 tablespoons margarine over medium-high heat. Add chicken; cook and stir until browned and no longer pink. Reduce heat to medium; stir in flour, salt, pepper, half-and-half and sherry. Cook until mixture boils and thickens, stirring constantly.
2. Stir in vegetables and 2 tablespoons Parmesan cheese. Cook an additional 4 to 6 minutes, or until thoroughly heated. Spoon hot mixture into ungreased 12 × 8-inch (2-quart) baking dish.
3. Remove crescent roll dough from can in rolled section; do not unroll. Cut roll into 12 slices; cut each slice in half. Arrange slice halves, curved side up, around outside of chicken mixture. Brush with 1 tablespoon melted margarine; sprinkle with 1 tablespoon Parmesan cheese. Sprinkle entire casserole with paprika.
4. Bake at 350°F. for 23 to 27 minutes, or until rolls are deep golden brown.

Yield: 6 servings

Nutrition Information Per Serving

Serving Size: ⅙ of Recipe • Calories 460 • Calories from Fat 220 • Total Fat 24 g
Saturated Fat 9 g • Cholesterol 90 mg • Sodium 700 mg • Dietary Fiber 2 g
Dietary Exchanges: 1½ Starch, 1 Vegetable, 3½ Lean Meat, 2½ Fat OR
1½ Carbohydrate, 1 Vegetable, 3½ Lean Meat, 2½ Fat

Crescent Chicken Newburg

Fruit 'n Nut–Stuffed Chicken Breasts

Prep Time: 30 minutes
(Ready in 1 hour)

Make It Special

Stir a generous amount of minced parsley into white rice cooked in pineapple juice. Place a mound of the rice in the center of each dinner plate. Slice each chicken roll and arrange the slices around the rice. Garnish with toasted walnut halves and serve slivers of fresh pineapple alongside.

Menu Suggestion

Serve with dry white wine, steamed asparagus and buttered carrot circles.

¼ cup pineapple juice
1 teaspoon honey
½ cup dried fruit bits
½ cup chopped walnuts, toasted*

4 boneless, skinless chicken breast halves
¼ cup unseasoned bread crumbs
2 tablespoons honey

1. Heat oven to 350°F. In small saucepan, combine pineapple juice and 1 teaspoon honey; add fruit bits. Bring to a boil. Reduce heat to low; cover and simmer 5 minutes, or until liquid is absorbed. Remove from heat; stir in ¼ cup of the chopped walnuts.
2. Place 1 chicken breast half between 2 pieces of plastic wrap or waxed paper. Working from center, gently pound chicken with flat side of meat mallet or rolling pin until about ¼ inch thick; remove wrap. Repeat with remaining chicken breast halves.
3. Place scant ¼ cup fruit mixture on center of each chicken breast. Bring about 1 inch of one end of chicken over mixture. Fold in sides; roll up jelly-roll fashion, pressing ends to seal. Secure with toothpicks if necessary.
4. In food processor bowl with metal blade or blender container, process remaining ¼ cup walnuts until ground. In small bowl, combine ground walnuts and bread crumbs. Brush chicken rolls with 2 tablespoons honey; roll in walnut mixture. Place chicken rolls in ungreased 8-inch square (1½-quart) baking dish.
5. Bake at 350°F. for 25 to 30 minutes, or until chicken is fork-tender and juices run clear.

Yield: 4 servings

*Tip: To toast walnuts, spread on cookie sheet; bake at 350°F. for 5 to 7 minutes, or until golden brown, stirring occasionally. Or, spread walnuts in thin layer in microwave-safe pan. Microwave on HIGH for 4 to 7 minutes, or until golden brown, stirring frequently.

Nutrition Information Per Serving
Serving Size: ¼ of Recipe • Calories 350 • Calories from Fat 110 • Total Fat 12 g Saturated Fat 2 g • Cholesterol 75 mg • Sodium 125 mg • Dietary Fiber 3 g Dietary Exchanges: 2 Fruit, 4 Lean Meat OR 2 Carbohydrate, 4 Lean Meat

Fruit 'n Nut–Stuffed Chicken Breasts

Lemon Chicken

Prep Time: 30 minutes

Ingredient Substitution

Boneless skinless chicken thighs work well in this pungent sauce, too. Substitute 8 thighs for the 4 breast halves.

Make It Special

Garnish with lemon wedges or thin curls of lemon zest.

Menu Suggestion

Serve the chicken on a bed of brown rice and accompany with steamed broccoli and a tossed salad.

Chicken
¾ cup finely crushed corn flakes cereal
½ teaspoon ginger
⅛ teaspoon pepper
1 egg white
1 teaspoon water
1 teaspoon soy sauce
4 boneless, skinless chicken breast halves

Sauce
½ cup chicken broth
1 tablespoon cornstarch
⅓ cup honey
3 tablespoons fresh lemon juice
1 teaspoon ketchup
⅛ teaspoon garlic powder
1 teaspoon grated lemon peel
2 green onions, cut into ½-inch pieces, including tops

1. Line cookie sheet with foil; place in oven. Heat oven to 450°F. In pie pan, combine crushed cereal, ginger and pepper; mix well. In small bowl, beat egg white, water and soy sauce until frothy. Brush both sides of chicken with egg white mixture. Place in pie pan; spoon cereal mixture over chicken to coat evenly.

2. Remove hot foil-lined cookie sheet from oven; arrange coated chicken on sheet. Bake at 450°F. for 15 to 20 minutes, or until chicken is fork-tender and juices run clear.

3. Meanwhile, in medium saucepan, combine broth and cornstarch; blend until smooth. Add honey, lemon juice, ketchup and garlic powder; mix well. Bring to a boil over medium-high heat, stirring constantly. Remove from heat; stir in lemon peel.

4. To serve, cut each chicken breast half crosswise into 6 or 7 pieces; arrange on 4 individual plates. Spoon sauce over chicken; sprinkle with green onions.

Yield: 4 servings

Nutrition Information Per Serving
Serving Size: ¼ of Recipe • Calories 310 • Calories from Fat 25 • Total Fat 3 g
Saturated Fat 1 g • Cholesterol 75 mg • Sodium 440 mg • Dietary Fiber 1 g
Dietary Exchanges: 1 Starch, 1½ Fruit, 4 Very Lean Meat OR
2½ Carbohydrate, 4 Very Lean Meat

Mediterranean Chicken and Garbanzos

Prep Time: 15 minutes
(Ready in 1 hour 15 minutes)

6 bone-in chicken breast halves, skin removed, if desired
2 tablespoons margarine or butter
½ teaspoon grated lemon peel
½ teaspoon ginger
¼ teaspoon cinnamon
¼ teaspoon pepper
⅛ teaspoon crushed red pepper flakes
2 garlic cloves, minced

1 (15-oz.) can garbanzo beans, drained, rinsed
1 (9-oz.) pkg. frozen baby lima beans in a pouch
½ cup kalamata or ripe olives, halved, pitted
¼ cup sliced green onions
2 tablespoons chopped fresh cilantro
¼ cup lemon juice
2 tablespoons olive oil or vegetable oil

1. Heat oven to 350°F. Place chicken breasts, meaty side up, in ungreased 13 × 9-inch (3-quart) baking dish.
2. In small saucepan, melt margarine over low heat. Stir in lemon peel, ginger, cinnamon, pepper, crushed red pepper flakes and garlic. Brush mixture over chicken. Bake uncovered at 350°F. for 45 minutes.
3. Meanwhile, in medium bowl, combine remaining ingredients. Spoon over chicken in baking dish. Cover; bake an additional 15 minutes, or until chicken is fork-tender and juices run clear. Arrange chicken on serving platter. Spoon bean mixture over chicken; drizzle with pan juices remaining in baking dish.

Yield: 6 servings

Nutrition Information Per Serving
Serving Size: ⅙ of Recipe • Calories 340 • Calories from Fat 130 • Total Fat 14 g
Saturated Fat 2 g • Cholesterol 75 mg • Sodium 370 mg • Dietary Fiber 6 g
Dietary Exchanges: 1½ Starch, 4 Lean Meat OR 1½ Carbohydrate, 4 Lean Meat

About Greek Olives

Greek kalamata olives, packed in a wine vinegar brine, are purple-black in color and typically found in Greek salad. To remove the pit, use a cherry pitter. Or, lay the side of a chef's knife over the olive and apply pressure to the knife with your hands. The pit should pop out.

Menu Suggestion

Accompany the chicken with warmed pita bread and a Greek salad of romaine lettuce, tomato wedges and feta cheese.

Mexicali Chicken and Rice Casserole

Prep Time: 20 minutes
(Ready in 1 hour 50 minutes)

1 tablespoon oil
1 cup chopped onions
½ cup chopped green bell pepper
1 garlic clove, minced
1 (15.5-oz.) can light red kidney beans, drained
1 (14.5-oz.) can whole tomatoes, undrained, cut up
1 (14½-oz.) can ready-to-serve chicken broth
1 (4.5-oz.) can diced green chiles, undrained

2 cups frozen whole kernel corn
¾ cup uncooked regular long-grain white rice
1 teaspoon chili powder
½ teaspoon salt
½ teaspoon pepper
2 tablespoons all-purpose flour
1 teaspoon garlic salt
3 teaspoons paprika
3 to 3½ lb. cut-up frying chicken, skin removed, if desired

1. Heat oven to 375°F. Heat oil in Dutch oven or large saucepan over medium-high heat until hot. Add onions, bell pepper and garlic; cook and stir until vegetables are tender. Add beans, tomatoes, broth, chiles, corn, rice, chili powder, salt and pepper; mix well. Pour mixture into ungreased 13 × 9-inch (3-quart) baking dish.

2. In plastic bag, combine flour, garlic salt and paprika; shake to mix. Add chicken; shake to coat. Place chicken pieces over rice mixture; press lightly into rice. Cover tightly with foil.

3. Bake at 375°F. for 1 hour to 1 hour 15 minutes, or until chicken is fork-tender and juices run clear. Remove foil; bake 15 minutes, or until chicken is browned.

Yield: 8 servings

Nutrition Information Per Serving

Serving Size: ⅛ of Recipe • Calories 330 • Calories from Fat 70 • Total Fat 8 g
Saturated Fat 2 g • Cholesterol 55 mg • Sodium 900 mg • Dietary Fiber 5 g
Dietary Exchanges: 2½ Starch, 2½ Lean Meat OR 2½ Carbohydrate, 2½ Lean Meat

Mustard Tarragon Chicken

Prep Time: 15 minutes
(Ready in 5 hours 15 minutes)

Marinade
1 (8-oz.) container sour cream
⅓ cup Dijon mustard
2 tablespoons sugar
2 tablespoons lemon juice
1 teaspoon dried tarragon
    leaves
½ teaspoon salt
⅛ teaspoon pepper

Chicken
6 boneless, skinless chicken
    breast halves
¾ cup plain bread crumbs
3 tablespoons margarine or
    butter, melted

1. In large bowl, combine all marinade ingredients; blend well. Add chicken to marinade, turning to coat. Cover bowl; refrigerate at least 4 hours or overnight.
2. Heat oven to 350°F. Lightly grease 13 × 9-inch (3-quart) baking dish. Remove chicken from marinade. Arrange in single layer in greased baking dish; spoon any remaining marinade evenly over chicken.
3. In small bowl, combine bread crumbs and margarine; blend well. Spoon evenly over chicken. Bake at 350°F. for 55 to 60 minutes, or until chicken is fork-tender and juices run clear.

Yield: 6 servings

Nutrition Information Per Serving
Serving Size: ⅙ of Recipe • Calories 350 • Calories from Fat 160 • Total Fat 18 g
Saturated Fat 7 g • Cholesterol 90 mg • Sodium 780 mg • Dietary Fiber 1 g
Dietary Exchanges: 1 Starch, 4 Lean Meat, 1 Fat OR
1 Carbohydrate, 4 Lean Meat, 1 Fat

About Tarragon

Tarragon has a slight licorice flavor. If the fresh version is available, strip the leaves from the stalk and use 1 tablespoon of the fresh chopped leaves instead of 1 teaspoon of the dried.

Healthy Hint

Substitute nonfat sour cream for regular to trim the fat content to 10 grams per serving and the calories to 290.

Menu Suggestion

Serve these saucy chicken breasts with baked white or sweet potatoes and steamed spinach.

Spicy Chicken Vegetable Pizzas

For hot oven grinders or hoagies, spoon the chicken and vegetable mixture onto split submarine sandwich rolls and bake until heated through. Or, heat the chicken mixture in the microwave oven and roll it into warmed flour tortillas.

Prep Time: 20 minutes

1 cup frozen corn, broccoli and red peppers, cooked, well drained

4 oz. (1 cup) shredded hot pepper Monterey Jack cheese

¾ cup shredded or chopped cooked chicken

½ cup chopped green onions

½ teaspoon dried oregano leaves

2 (6-inch) prebaked Italian bread shells

1. Heat oven to 425°F. In medium bowl, combine vegetables, cheese, chicken, green onions and oregano; toss to combine. Place bread shells on ungreased cookie sheet. Spoon vegetable mixture evenly on bread shells.

2. Bake at 425°F. for 5 to 6 minutes, or until thoroughly heated and cheese is melted.

Yield: 2 servings

Nutrition Information Per Serving

Serving Size: ½ of Recipe • Calories 680 • Calories from Fat 230 • Total Fat 26 g
Saturated Fat 13 g • Cholesterol 105 mg • Sodium 970 mg • Dietary Fiber 4 g
Dietary Exchanges: 4 Starch, 1 Vegetable, 4½ Lean Meat, 2½ Fat OR
4 Carbohydrate, 1 Vegetable, 4½ Lean Meat, 2½ Fat

Oven Chicken Cordon Bleu

Prep Time: 20 minutes
(Ready in 50 minutes)

- 4 boneless, skinless chicken breast halves
- 2 teaspoons Dijon mustard
- 4 teaspoons chopped fresh chives
- 4 very thin slices cooked lean ham (about ¾ oz. each)
- 4 very thin slices reduced-fat Swiss cheese (about ¾ oz. each)
- 1 egg white
- 1 tablespoon water
- ⅓ cup finely crushed corn flakes or bran flakes cereal
- ¼ teaspoon paprika

1. Heat oven to 375°F. Spray 8-inch square (1½-quart) baking dish with nonstick cooking spray. Place 1 chicken breast half between 2 pieces of plastic wrap or waxed paper. Working from center, gently pound chicken with flat side of meat mallet or rolling pin until about ¼ inch thick; remove wrap. Repeat with remaining chicken breast halves.

2. Spread each chicken breast half with ½ teaspoon mustard; sprinkle each with 1 teaspoon chives. Cut ham and cheese slices to fit chicken. Top each chicken breast half with ham and cheese slice. Roll up, tucking ends inside.

3. In shallow bowl, combine egg white and water; beat slightly. Place cereal crumbs in shallow dish. Coat chicken rolls with egg white mixture; roll in crumbs. Place in sprayed dish; sprinkle with paprika.

4. Bake at 375°F. for 25 to 30 minutes, or until chicken is fork-tender and juices run clear.

Yield: 4 servings

Nutrition Information Per Serving

Serving Size: ¼ of Recipe • Calories 250 • Calories from Fat 60 • Total Fat 7 g
Saturated Fat 3 g • Cholesterol 95 mg • Sodium 790 mg • Dietary Fiber 0 g
Dietary Exchanges: ½ Starch, 5 Very Lean Meat OR
½ Carbohydrate, 5 Very Lean Meat

Recipe Fact

For the classic chicken cordon bleu, the stuffed chicken breasts are browned in oil in a skillet before being transferred to the oven. This version is baked instead of fried to reduce calories and fat.

Make It Special

Arrange individual chives (with the flowers attached, if available) in a decorative pattern atop each serving. Chive flowers, like the flowers of most other herbs, are edible; they taste like chives. The stalks of chives that have gone to flower, however, are tough and fibrous.

Menu Suggestion

Rice pilaf and steamed asparagus spears round out this meal.

Oven-Fried Chicken

Recipe Fact

A crisp, tender crust forms while the chicken bakes, yielding a lighter, updated alternative to deep-fried chicken.

About Poultry Seasoning

The exact components of poultry seasoning vary from brand to brand, but the blend usually contains sage, marjoram and thyme, all of which go very well with poultry.

1 cup mashed potato flakes
1 teaspoon salt
¼ teaspoon pepper
¼ to ½ teaspoon poultry seasoning

1 egg, slightly beaten
1 teaspoon lemon juice
3 to 3½ lb. cut-up frying chicken, skin removed

1. Heat oven to 375°F. In plastic bag, combine potato flakes, salt, pepper and poultry seasoning; shake to mix. In shallow bowl, combine egg and lemon juice. Dip chicken in egg mixture. Add to flour mixture in bag; shake to coat. Place chicken in ungreased 15 × 10 × 1-inch baking pan.

2. Bake at 375°F. for 45 to 60 minutes, or until chicken is fork-tender and juices run clear.

Yield: 4 servings

Nutrition Information Per Serving

Serving Size: ¼ of Recipe • Calories 320 • Calories from Fat 100 • Total Fat 11 g
Saturated Fat 3 g • Cholesterol 165 mg • Sodium 690 mg • Dietary Fiber 1 g
Dietary Exchanges: 1 Starch, 5 Very Lean Meat, 1 Fat OR
1 Carbohydrate, 5 Very Lean Meat, 1 Fat

Oven-Fried Chicken

Roast Chicken

Prep Time: 30 minutes
(Ready in 1 hour 35 minutes)

1 (3- to 3½-lb.) whole frying
   chicken
2 tablespoons margarine or
   butter, melted

2 tablespoons white wine
   Worcestershire sauce

1. Heat oven to 375°F. Remove giblets from body cavity. Rinse chicken inside and out with cold water; drain. Pat dry with paper towels. Using string, tie legs and tail together. Close neck cavity by bringing loose skin over opening and holding in place with metal skewer. Twist wing tips under back.

2. Place chicken, breast side up, on rack in shallow roasting pan. In small bowl, combine margarine and Worcestershire sauce; brush chicken with half of mixture. **Do not cover or add water.**

3. Bake at 375°F. for 55 to 65 minutes, brushing with remaining margarine mixture halfway through baking. Untie chicken legs about 10 minutes before end of baking time. Chicken is done when fork-tender, juices run clear and drumstick moves easily up and down and twists in socket. Let stand 5 to 10 minutes before carving.

Yield: 4 servings

Nutrition Information Per Serving

Serving Size: ¼ of Recipe • Calories 300 • Calories from Fat 140 • Total Fat 16 g
Saturated Fat 4 g • Cholesterol 115 mg • Sodium 260 mg • Dietary Fiber 0 g
Dietary Exchanges: 5 Lean Meat

Kitchen Tip

Unwaxed dental floss makes a convenient string for trussing the bird.

Kitchen Tip

To test for doneness, pierce the skin between the thigh and the body. Clear juices indicate doneness; if the juice still runs pink, roast the bird a little longer.

Menu Suggestion

Roast chicken is a traditional centerpiece for a family dinner. Accompany it with fresh cranberry relish, buttered Brussels sprouts, mashed potatoes and tender green peas. Finish the meal with an old-fashioned homemade dessert, such as apple crisp, pumpkin pie or bread pudding.

Roasted Apricot Chicken with Pecan Stuffing

Prep Time: 40 minutes
(Ready in 2 hours 50 minutes)

1 (3- to 5-lb.) whole roasting or frying chicken	½ cup chopped pecans
3 to 4 cups stuffing mix (not cubes)	½ cup golden raisins
Margarine or butter	3 tablespoons margarine or butter, melted
Water	¼ cup apricot preserves
	¼ teaspoon cinnamon

1. Heat oven to 325°F. Remove giblets from body cavity. Rinse chicken inside and out with cold water; drain. Pat dry with paper towels. In medium bowl, prepare stuffing mix with margarine and water according to package directions. Stir in pecans and raisins. Fill cavity of chicken loosely with stuffing. Spoon remaining stuffing into small baking dish; cover with foil and refrigerate. Using string, tie legs and tail together. Close neck cavity by bringing loose skin over opening and holding in place with metal skewer. Twist wing tips under back.

2. Place chicken, breast side up, on rack in shallow roasting pan. Brush chicken with 1 tablespoon of the melted margarine. Bake at 325°F. for 1½ hours.

3. In small bowl, combine remaining 2 tablespoons melted margarine with apricot preserves and cinnamon. Remove chicken from oven; brush apricot mixture generously over chicken. Remove reserved stuffing from refrigerator. Place chicken and reserved stuffing in oven.

4. Bake chicken an additional 30 to 40 minutes, brushing occasionally with remaining apricot mixture. Bake reserved stuffing until thoroughly heated.* Untie legs about 10 minutes before end of baking time. Chicken is done when fork-tender, juices run clear and drumstick moves easily up and down and twists in socket. Let stand

Recipe Fact

Letting a whole roasted chicken or turkey stand for 10 to 20 minutes prior to carving gives the juices time to redistribute and makes the meat easier to slice.

Kitchen Tip

Remove all the stuffing from the chicken before serving. Otherwise, the stuffing in the cavity cools at a different rate from the meat, leading to ideal conditions for bacterial growth. Refrigerate left-over stuffing and chicken separately, as soon after serving as possible.

Ingredient Substitution

Walnuts or almonds can stand in for the pecans; chopped dried apricots, pitted prunes or mixed dried (not candied) fruit can replace some or all of the raisins.

Menu Suggestion

Serve the chicken with buttered green beans, a big tossed salad and cranberry muffins.

5 to 10 minutes before carving. Bring any remaining apricot mixture to a boil; serve with chicken.

Yield: 6 servings

*Tip: Stuffing in baking dish will be drier than stuffing in chicken. For moister stuffing, add 2 tablespoons chicken broth or water to stuffing in baking dish before baking.

Nutrition Information Per Serving

Serving Size: ⅙ of Recipe • Calories 730 • Calories from Fat 380 • Total Fat 42 g
Saturated Fat 9 g • Cholesterol 135 mg • Sodium 720 mg • Dietary Fiber 3 g
Dietary Exchanges: 1 Starch, 2 Fruit, 6 Lean Meat, 5 Fat OR
3 Carbohydrate, 6 Lean Meat, 5 Fat

Sage and Rosemary Roast Chicken

Prep Time: 15 minutes
(Ready in 1 hour 45 minutes)

3 to 3½ lb. cut-up or quartered frying chicken
4 medium baking potatoes, unpeeled, quartered
1 bunch (about 8) green onions, trimmed, cut into 2-inch pieces
½ teaspoon dried sage leaves
½ teaspoon dried rosemary leaves, crushed
¼ teaspoon salt
¼ teaspoon coarsely ground black pepper

1. Heat oven to 375°F. Arrange chicken, potatoes and green onions in ungreased 13 × 9-inch (3-quart) baking dish. Sprinkle with sage, rosemary, salt and pepper.
2. Bake at 375°F. for 1¼ to 1½ hours, or until chicken is fork-tender, its juices run clear, and potatoes are tender.

Yield: 4 servings

Nutrition Information Per Serving

Serving Size: ¼ of Recipe • Calories 590 • Calories from Fat 190 • Total Fat 21 g
Saturated Fat 6 g • Cholesterol 135 mg • Sodium 280 mg • Dietary Fiber 6 g
Dietary Exchanges: 3½ Starch, 5½ Lean Meat, 1 Fat OR
3½ Carbohydrate, 5½ Lean Meat, 1 Fat

About Rosemary

"Rosemary for remembrance" goes the old saying, and a gift of rosemary was said to confer happiness upon newlyweds. The piney herb has a strong, resinous flavor. To cook with fresh rosemary, strip the needle-like leaves from the woody stem.

Make-Ahead Tip

If you wish to quarter the potatoes ahead of time, immediately submerge the cut pieces into a bowl of cold water until cooking time to prevent discoloration.

Tomatillo Chicken Enchiladas

Prep Time: 30 minutes
(Ready in 1 hour 10 minutes)

Salsa
2 lb. fresh tomatillos*
1 cup chopped onions
3 serrano chile peppers, seeded, chopped
3 garlic cloves, crushed
1/4 cup lime juice
1/4 cup chopped fresh cilantro
1/2 teaspoon salt

Enchiladas
2 cups shredded cooked chicken
8 oz. (2 cups) shredded hot pepper Monterey Jack cheese or Monterey Jack cheese
1/2 cup chopped green onions
1/2 teaspoon cumin
1/2 teaspoon chili powder
1/4 teaspoon salt
12 (6-inch) soft corn tortillas, heated

1. Remove husks from tomatillos; rinse. Place tomatillos in large saucepan; add enough water to cover. Bring to a boil. Reduce heat to medium; cover and cook 8 to 10 minutes, or until tender. Drain.
2. Place tomatillos in food processor bowl with metal blade or blender container; process with on/off pulses just until smooth.** In large bowl, combine tomatillos and all remaining salsa ingredients; mix well. Spread 1 cup of the salsa over bottom of ungreased 13 × 9-inch (3-quart) baking dish.
3. Heat oven to 350°F. In large bowl, combine chicken, 1 cup of the cheese, 1 cup of the salsa, green onions, cumin, chili powder and 1/4 teaspoon salt; mix well. Spoon 2 heaping tablespoons chicken mixture down center of each tortilla; roll up. Place, seam side down, over salsa in baking dish. Spoon 1/2 cup of the salsa over filled enchiladas. Cover.
4. Bake at 350°F. for 30 to 35 minutes, or until thoroughly heated. Top with remaining salsa and cheese.

Bake an additional 2 to 3 minutes, or until cheese is melted.

Yield: 6 servings

*Tip: Three 11-oz. cans tomatillos, drained, can be substituted for fresh tomatillos. Omit step 1.

**After tomatillos are processed in blender, they can be refrigerated up to 1 day or frozen up to 3 months.

Nutrition Information Per Serving

Serving Size: ⅙ of Recipe • Calories 410 • Calories from Fat 150 • Total Fat 17 g
Saturated Fat 8 g • Cholesterol 75 mg • Sodium 600 mg • Dietary Fiber 6 g
Dietary Exchanges: 2 Starch, 1 Vegetable, 3 Lean Meat, 1½ Fat OR
2 Carbohydrate, 1 Vegetable, 3 Lean Meat, 1½ Fat

Spicy Honey-Glazed Drumettes

Prep Time: 15 minutes
(Ready in 1 hour 30 minutes)

3 lb. chicken drumettes
1 cup honey
½ cup ketchup
¼ cup soy sauce

¼ teaspoon ground red pepper (cayenne)
¼ teaspoon ginger

1. Heat oven to 375°F. Arrange drumettes in ungreased 13 × 9-inch (3-quart) baking dish. In small bowl, combine remaining ingredients; blend well. Pour over drumettes.
2. Bake at 375°F. for 1 to 1¼ hours, or until drumettes are glazed and no longer pink, basting occasionally.

Yield: 8 servings

Nutrition Information Per Serving

Serving Size: ⅛ of Recipe • Calories 350 • Calories from Fat 120 • Total Fat 13 g
Saturated Fat 4 g • Cholesterol 55 mg • Sodium 750 mg • Dietary Fiber 0 g
Dietary Exchanges: 3 Fruit, 3 Lean Meat, 1 Fat OR
3 Carbohydrate, 3 Lean Meat, 1 Fat

About Drumettes

A drumette is the part of the chicken wing that resembles a little drumstick.

Menu Suggestion

Serve the drumettes as an appetizer, using the sauce for dipping, or as a main course with rice, carrot and celery sticks, and wedges of iceberg lettuce.

Light Sour Cream Chicken Enchiladas

While you're waiting for the enchiladas to cook, serve an appetizer of baked tortilla chips with purchased or homemade salsa. Accompany the enchiladas with tomato slices on a bed of curly-leaf lettuce or a quick salad made of black beans, corn kernels (fresh cooked or canned, drained), chopped red onion, and cilantro or parsley, all tossed with a vinaigrette dressing.

Make It Special

For lovers of the hot and spicy, serve the enchiladas with bottled chile pepper sauce, extra-spicy salsa or chopped jalapeños.

Prep Time: 15 minutes
(Ready in 45 minutes)

1 (8-oz.) container light sour cream

1 (8-oz.) container nonfat plain yogurt

1 ($10^3/_4$-oz.) can condensed 99%-fat-free cream of chicken soup with $^1/_3$ less sodium

1 (4.5-oz.) can diced green chiles, undrained

12 (6- or 7-inch) white corn or flour tortillas

4 oz. (1 cup) shredded reduced-fat Cheddar cheese

$1^1/_2$ cups chopped cooked chicken

$^1/_4$ cup sliced green onions

1. Heat oven to 350°F. Spray 13 × 9-inch (3-quart) baking dish with nonstick cooking spray. In medium bowl, combine sour cream, yogurt, soup and chiles; mix well.

2. Spoon about 3 tablespoons sour cream mixture down center of each tortilla. Reserve $^1/_4$ cup of the cheese; sprinkle tortillas with remaining cheese, chicken and green onions. Roll up; place in sprayed dish. Spoon remaining sour cream mixture over tortillas. Cover with foil.

3. Bake at 350°F. for 25 to 30 minutes, or until hot and bubbly. Remove foil; sprinkle with reserved $^1/_4$ cup cheese. Bake uncovered for an additional 5 minutes, or until cheese is melted. If desired, garnish with shredded lettuce and chopped tomatoes.

Yield: 6 servings

Nutrition Information Per Serving

Serving Size: $^1/_6$ of Recipe • Calories 350 • Calories from Fat 100 • Total Fat 11 g
Saturated Fat 5 g • Cholesterol 55 mg • Sodium 740 mg • Dietary Fiber 3 g
Dietary Exchanges: 2 Starch, 1 Vegetable, 2 Lean Meat, 1 Fat OR
2 Carbohydrate, 1 Vegetable, 2 Lean Meat, 1 Fat

Light Sour Cream Chicken Enchiladas

Grilled and

Broiled Entrees

Recipes for grilled and broiled poultry are ideal for healthy cooking because they generally call for little or no added fat. A crisp, golden-brown exterior and juicy, savory interior characterize chicken cooked by these techniques. As a big payback for the more careful monitoring required, chicken emerges from the grill or the broiler in about half the time of other cooking methods.

Grilled and Broiled Entrees

Previous page: Teriyaki Grilled Chicken Kabobs page 215

Teriyaki Grilled Chicken Kabobs

Prep Time: 30 minutes
(Ready in 2 hours 30 minutes)

Marinade
2 tablespoons brown sugar
3 tablespoons soy sauce
2 tablespoons dry sherry
1 tablespoon oil
¼ teaspoon ginger
⅛ teaspoon garlic powder

Kabobs
8 boneless, skinless chicken thighs
1 large red bell pepper, cut into 8 pieces
1 medium zucchini, cut into 8 pieces
8 (1- to 2-inch) chunks fresh pineapple or 8 canned pineapple chunks

1. In 12 × 8-inch (2-quart) baking dish or large resealable plastic bag, combine all marinade ingredients. Cut chicken thighs in half; add to marinade. Cover dish or seal bag. Refrigerate at least 2 hours to marinate, turning chicken once.

2. Heat grill. Drain chicken, reserving marinade. Alternately thread chicken, bell pepper, zucchini and pineapple onto four 12-inch metal skewers.

3. When ready to grill, place kabobs on gas grill over medium heat or on charcoal grill 4 to 6 inches from medium-high coals. Cook 15 to 20 minutes, or until chicken is no longer pink, turning often and brushing frequently with reserved marinade. Discard any remaining marinade.

Yield: 4 kabobs

Tip: To broil, place kabobs on broiler pan and broil 4 to 6 inches from heat using times provided above as a guide.

Nutrition Information Per Serving
Serving Size: 1 Kabob • Calories 280 • Calories from Fat 120 • Total Fat 13 g
Saturated Fat 3 g • Cholesterol 100 mg • Sodium 300 mg • Dietary Fiber 2 g
Dietary Exchanges: ½ Fruit, 1 Vegetable, 4 Lean Meat OR
½ Carbohydrate, 1 Vegetable, 4 Lean Meat

Recipe Fact
Teriyaki refers to meat or shellfish that has been marinated in a flavorful mixture of soy sauce, sake or sherry, sugar, ginger and seasonings.

Kitchen Tip
To prepare a fresh pineapple, slice off the leafy top. Cut the fruit in half lengthwise. Cut each half into four lengthwise wedges, then slice off the thin piece of tough core that runs the length of each wedge. Run a sharp knife between the bumpy skin and the fruit to release the flesh. Use a sharp vegetable peeler or paring knife to remove any prickly eyes that remain in the flesh, then cut the fruit into chunks.

Apricot-Glazed Chicken Breasts with Almond Couscous

30 min. or less • low-fat

Ingredient Substitution

Use peach preserves in place of the apricot.

Menu Suggestion

Steamed broccoli with sliced water chestnuts would make a good side dish, along with whole wheat dinner rolls.

Prep Time: 25 minutes

Chicken
4 boneless, skinless chicken breast halves
½ teaspoon garlic powder
¼ teaspoon pepper
⅛ teaspoon ground red pepper (cayenne)
2 tablespoons apricot preserves

Couscous
1 cup chicken broth
1 tablespoon margarine or butter
1 cup uncooked couscous
2 tablespoons slivered almonds, toasted

1. Place 1 chicken breast half between 2 pieces of plastic wrap or waxed paper. Working from center, gently pound chicken with flat side of meat mallet or rolling pin until about ¼ inch thick; remove wrap. Repeat with remaining chicken breast halves.

2. In small bowl, combine garlic powder, pepper and ground red pepper; mix well. Sprinkle on both sides of chicken. Arrange chicken on broiler pan.

3. Broil 4 to 6 inches from heat for 6 to 10 minutes, or until chicken is fork-tender and juices run clear. Brush with half of apricot preserves. Broil 1 minute, or until bubbly. Brush with remaining preserves.

4. Meanwhile, in medium saucepan, bring broth and margarine to a boil. Stir in couscous and almonds. Remove from heat; cover. Let stand 5 minutes.

Yield: 4 servings

Nutrition Information Per Serving

Serving Size: ¼ of Recipe • Calories 390 • Calories from Fat 70 • Total Fat 8 g
Saturated Fat 2 g • Cholesterol 75 mg • Sodium 300 mg • Dietary Fiber 3 g
Dietary Exchanges: 2 Starch, 1 Fruit, 4 Very Lean Meat, 1 Fat OR
3 Carbohydrate, 4 Very Lean Meat, 1 Fat

Cajun Grilled Chicken with Fresh Tomato Relish

Prep Time: 20 minutes

Relish
2 medium tomatoes, chopped
½ cup chopped green onions
⅓ cup chopped celery
¼ teaspoon salt
¼ teaspoon hot pepper sauce

Chicken
4 boneless, skinless chicken breast halves
1 tablespoon dried Cajun seasoning

Grill Directions: 1. Heat grill. In medium bowl, combine all relish ingredients; mix well.

2. Coat both sides of each chicken breast half evenly with Cajun seasoning. When ready to grill, oil grill rack. Place chicken on gas grill over medium heat or on charcoal grill 4 to 6 inches from medium coals. Cook 8 to 10 minutes, or until chicken is fork-tender and juices run clear, turning once. Serve relish with chicken.

Yield: 4 servings

Broiler Directions: 1. Prepare relish and coat chicken with Cajun seasoning as directed above. Place chicken on broiler pan.

2. Broil 4 to 6 inches from heat for 8 to 10 minutes, or until chicken is fork-tender and juices run clear, turning once. Serve relish with chicken.

Nutrition Information Per Serving

Serving Size: ¼ of Recipe • Calories 160 • Calories from Fat 30 • Total Fat 3.5 g
Saturated Fat 1 g • Cholesterol 75 mg • Sodium 540 mg • Dietary Fiber 1 g
Dietary Exchanges: 1 Vegetable, 4 Very Lean Meat

About Cajun Seasoning

Dry Cajun seasoning, popularized by chef Paul Prudhomme and other Louisiana cooks, is a spicy blend that usually contains ground chiles, black pepper, cumin and other flavorings.

Menu Suggestion

Accompany the spicy chicken with cucumber spears, homemade potato salad and cornbread. End the meal with watermelon wedges and cookies.

Chicken Breasts with Veggie Salsa

About Thyme

Thyme's warm, rich flavor makes it one of the most versatile herbs to use fresh or dried with poultry, meat, fish and seafood; in soups and chowders; with many vegetables and in sauces and herb butters.

Menu Suggestion

Warm breadsticks and crisp lettuce wedges topped with salad dressing are easy accompaniments.

Prep Time: 25 minutes

Chicken
1 tablespoon margarine or butter, softened
1 tablespoon honey
1 teaspoon chopped fresh thyme or ¼ teaspoon dried thyme leaves
4 boneless, skinless chicken breast halves

Salsa
1½ cups shredded carrots
1½ cups shredded zucchini
1 cup sliced fresh mushrooms
1 cup chopped onions
1 tablespoon margarine or butter
½ teaspoon chopped fresh thyme or ⅛ teaspoon dried thyme leaves
¼ teaspoon salt
3 to 4 drops hot pepper sauce

1. Heat grill. In small bowl, combine 1 tablespoon margarine, honey and 1 teaspoon thyme; blend well.

2. When ready to grill, place chicken on gas grill over medium heat or on charcoal grill 4 to 6 inches from medium coals. Cook 8 to 10 minutes, or until chicken is fork-tender and juices run clear, turning once and brushing with honey mixture during last 5 minutes of cooking.

3. In large skillet, combine all salsa ingredients. Cook and stir over medium-high heat 3 to 4 minutes, or until vegetables are crisp-tender. Serve chicken over salsa.

Yield: 4 servings

Tip: To broil, place chicken on broiler pan and broil 4 to 6 inches from heat using times provided above as a guide.

Nutrition Information Per Serving

Serving Size: ¼ of Recipe • Calories 250 • Calories from Fat 80 • Total Fat 9 g
Saturated Fat 2 g • Cholesterol 75 mg • Sodium 280 mg • Dietary Fiber 3 g
Dietary Exchanges: 3 Vegetable, 3 Lean Meat

Chicken Breasts with Veggie Salsa

Cranberry-Glazed Chicken

Serve the chicken with mashed potatoes, steamed broccoli and a simple salad of chopped cucumber, tomato and red onion in vinaigrette. Apple pie à la mode would make a fine dessert.

Prep Time: 1 hour 15 minutes

Glaze
1 tablespoon oil
¼ cup chopped onion
½ cup ketchup
¼ cup firmly packed brown sugar
1 (8-oz.) can jellied cranberry sauce

Chicken
3 to 3½ lb. cut-up or quartered frying chicken, skin removed, if desired

Grill Directions: 1. Heat grill. In medium saucepan, heat oil over medium-high heat until hot. Add onion; cook and stir until crisp-tender. Stir in ketchup, brown sugar and cranberry sauce. Cook over low heat until cranberry sauce is melted, stirring occasionally.
2. When ready to grill, place chicken on gas grill over low heat or on charcoal grill 4 to 6 inches from medium coals. Cook 45 to 60 minutes, or until chicken is fork-tender and juices run clear, turning often and brushing frequently with glaze during last 15 minutes of cooking. Heat any remaining glaze to a boil; serve with chicken.

Yield: 4 servings

Oven Directions: 1. Heat oven to 350°F. Prepare sauce as directed above. Place chicken, skin side down, in ungreased 13 × 9-inch baking dish. Bake at 350°F. for 30 minutes. Using spoon, remove most of the pan juices; turn chicken.
2. Return to oven; bake an additional 15 to 25 minutes, or until chicken is fork-tender and juices run clear, brushing frequently with glaze during last 15 minutes of cooking. Heat any remaining glaze to a boil; serve with chicken.

Cranberry-Glazed Chicken

Nutrition Information Per Serving
Serving Size: ¼ of Recipe • Calories 580 • Calories from Fat 230 • Total Fat 25 g
Saturated Fat 6 g • Cholesterol 135 mg • Sodium 510 mg • Dietary Fiber 1 g
Dietary Exchanges: 3 Fruit, 6 Lean Meat, 1½ Fat OR
3 Carbohydrate, 6 Lean Meat, 1½ Fat

Citrus Barbecue Glazed Chicken

Prep Time: 1 hour 10 minutes

Glaze
½ cup barbecue sauce
¼ cup orange juice
2 tablespoons brown sugar
2 tablespoons lemon juice

Chicken
3 to 3½ lb. cut-up or quartered frying chicken, skin removed, if desired

Grill Directions: 1. Heat grill. In small saucepan, combine all glaze ingredients. Bring to a boil, stirring occasionally. Remove from heat.
2. When ready to grill, place chicken, skin side down, on gas grill over low heat or on charcoal grill 4 to 6 inches from medium coals. Cook 45 to 60 minutes, or until chicken is fork-tender and juices run clear, turning often and brushing frequently with glaze during last 15 minutes of cooking. Heat any remaining glaze to a boil; serve with chicken.

Yield: 4 servings

Oven and Broiler Directions: 1. Heat oven to 350°F. Prepare glaze as directed above. Place chicken, skin side up, in ungreased 13 × 9-inch (3-quart) baking dish. Bake at 350°F. for 45 to 60 minutes, or until chicken is fork-tender and juices run clear.
2. Transfer chicken, skin side up, to broiler pan. Broil 4 to 6 inches from heat for 2 to 4 minutes, brushing frequently with glaze. Heat any remaining glaze to a boil; serve with chicken.

Nutrition Information Per Serving

Serving Size: ¼ of Recipe • Calories 420 • Calories from Fat 200 • Total Fat 22 g
Saturated Fat 6 g • Cholesterol 135 mg • Sodium 390 mg • Dietary Fiber 0 g
Dietary Exchanges: 1 Fruit, 6 Lean Meat, ½ Fat OR
1 Carbohydrate, 6 Lean Meat, ½ Fat

Grilled Barbecue Chicken Pizza

Prep Time: 20 minutes

2 cups cubed cooked chicken	**8 oz. (2 cups) shredded**
½ cup barbecue sauce	**Monterey Jack cheese**
1 teaspoon chili powder	**¼ cup finely chopped onion**
1 (16-oz.) prebaked Italian	**¼ cup chopped green bell**
bread shell	**pepper**

Grill Directions: 1. Heat grill. In small bowl, combine chicken, barbecue sauce and chili powder; spread evenly on bread shell. Sprinkle with cheese, onion and bell pepper.
2. When ready to grill, place pizza directly on gas grill over medium heat or on charcoal grill 4 to 6 inches from medium coals. Cover grill; cook 10 minutes, or until bottom of pizza is crisp and cheese is melted.

Yield: 8 servings

Oven Directions: 1. Heat oven to 450°F. Prepare pizza as directed above. Place on ungreased cookie sheet.
2. Bake at 450°F. for 12 minutes, or until bottom of pizza is crisp and cheese is melted.

Nutrition Information Per Serving
Serving Size: ⅛ of Recipe • Calories 340 • Calories from Fat 140 • Total Fat 15 g
Saturated Fat 7 g • Cholesterol 60 mg • Sodium 610 mg • Dietary Fiber 1 g
Dietary Exchanges: 2 Starch, 2½ Lean Meat, 2 Fat OR
2 Carbohydrate, 2½ Lean Meat, 2 Fat

About Bread Shells

Prebaked Italian bread shells, available at most supermarkets, make it easy to turn a few simple ingredients into a satisfying pizza. Topped or not, the bread shells are best heated.

Recipe Variation

Substitute spaghetti sauce for the barbecue sauce and fresh mozzarella for the Monterey Jack. (This variation reduces fat by 4 grams.)

Menu Suggestion

Offer beer, iced tea or red wine with this casual entree, accompanied by a green salad and fresh raw vegetables with dip.

Grilled Chicken Breasts with Georgia Peach Salsa

Prep Time: 30 minutes

Recipe Fact

Salsa is the Mexican word for "sauce." The sauces—either fresh or cooked—may consist of chopped vegetables, fruits or both, and seasonings that lend a hot, mild, sweet or tart taste. One ingredient is common to most salsas: chiles.

Ingredient Substitution

Use nectarines or plums in place of the peaches.

Salsa
1 cup chopped peeled ripe peaches
1 tablespoon fresh lime juice
2 teaspoons brown sugar
½ cup diced red bell pepper
2 tablespoons thinly sliced green onions

1 tablespoon minced jalapeño chile pepper
Dash salt

Chicken
4 boneless, skinless chicken breast halves
⅛ teaspoon salt
⅛ teaspoon pepper

1. Heat grill. In medium bowl, combine peaches, lime juice and brown sugar; mix well. Stir in bell pepper, green onions, chile pepper and dash of salt.

2. Place 1 chicken breast half between 2 pieces of plastic wrap or waxed paper. Working from center, gently pound with flat side of meat mallet or rolling pin until about ¼ inch thick; remove wrap. Repeat with remaining chicken breast halves.

3. When ready to grill, oil grill rack. Lightly sprinkle chicken with ⅛ teaspoon salt and pepper. Place chicken on oiled rack on gas grill over medium heat or on charcoal grill 4 to 6 inches from medium coals. Cook 6 to 10 minutes, or until chicken is fork-tender and juices run clear, turning once. Serve with salsa.

Yield: 4 servings

Tip: To broil, place chicken on broiler pan and broil 4 to 6 inches from heat using times provided above as a guide.

Nutrition Information Per Serving
Serving Size: ¼ of Recipe • Calories 160 • Calories from Fat 25 • Total Fat 3 g
Saturated Fat 1 g • Cholesterol 75 mg • Sodium 180 mg • Dietary Fiber 1 g
Dietary Exchanges: ½ Fruit, 4 Very Lean Meat OR
½ Carbohydrate, 4 Very Lean Meat

Grilled Rosemary Chicken

low-fat

Prep Time: 35 minutes

6 boneless chicken breast halves (with skin)
12 sprigs fresh rosemary or 2 tablespoons dried rosemary leaves, crushed
12 sprigs fresh oregano or 2 tablespoons dried oregano leaves, crushed
6 garlic cloves, halved lengthwise

Grill Directions: 1. Heat grill. Loosen skin on one edge of each chicken breast half. Under the skin of each, place 2 sprigs rosemary or 1 teaspoon dried rosemary, 2 sprigs oregano or 1 teaspoon dried oregano and 2 garlic clove halves. Smooth skin over seasonings and chicken breast halves.

2. When ready to grill, place chicken on gas grill over medium heat or on charcoal grill 4 to 6 inches from medium coals. Cook 10 to 12 minutes, or until chicken is fork-tender and juices run clear, turning once halfway through cooking. Cool slightly.

3. To serve, remove skin and seasonings from chicken. Slice crosswise into strips. Arrange on serving platter. Garnish as desired.

Yield: 6 servings

Broiler Directions: 1. Prepare chicken as directed above. Place chicken on broiler pan.

2. Broil 4 to 6 inches from heat for 10 to 12 minutes, or until chicken is fork-tender and juices run clear, turning once halfway through cooking. Cool slightly. Serve as directed above.

Nutrition Information Per Serving

Serving Size: 1/6 of Recipe • Calories 190 • Calories from Fat 70 • Total Fat 8 g
Saturated Fat 2 g • Cholesterol 80 mg • Sodium 70 mg • Dietary Fiber 0 g
Dietary Exchanges: 4 Very Lean Meat, 1 Fat

Make-Ahead Tip

The chicken can be grilled up to two days ahead of time, refrigerated and served cold.

Menu Suggestion

This fragrant herbed chicken works well as a picnic meal. Be sure to keep it cold until meal-time in a well-insulated cooler, along with plenty of thirst-quenching beverages. Take along sandwich rolls and carrot and celery sticks in self-sealing plastic bags. For a simple picnic dessert, try kiwi fruit the way it's often served in its native New Zealand: Cut the rinsed fruit in half, and eat the green flesh right out of the skin with a spoon.

Indonesian Chicken

Prep Time: 1 hour 10 minutes
(Ready in 7 hours 10 minutes)

Recipe Fact

Like many Asian recipes, this highly seasoned chicken combines flavor opposites to yield an entree that practically explodes with taste. Here, the recipe mingles sweet (coconut milk), sour (vinegar) and salty (soy sauce, fish sauce) with spicy (curry, hot pepper flakes) and crunchy (chopped peanuts).

About Fish Sauce

Fish sauce, **nam pla** (Thai) or **nuoc mam** (Vietnamese) is a fermented sauce with a pungent odor and distinctive flavor important to many Asian dishes. Purchase it at an Asian market or in the international aisles of large grocery stores.

Marinade
1 (14-oz.) can coconut milk
2 tablespoons fish sauce
2 tablespoons rice vinegar or cider vinegar
1 teaspoon soy sauce
¼ cup finely chopped peanuts
2 garlic cloves, minced

2 to 3 teaspoons curry powder
1 teaspoon crushed red pepper flakes

Chicken
3 to 3½ lb. cut-up frying chicken, skin removed, if desired

Grill Directions: **1.** In 12 × 8-inch (2-quart) glass baking dish or large resealable plastic bag, combine all marinade ingredients; blend well. Add chicken; turn to coat. Cover dish or seal bag; refrigerate at least 6 hours or overnight, turning occasionally.
2. Heat grill. When ready to grill, drain chicken, reserving marinade. Place chicken on gas grill over low heat or on charcoal grill 4 to 6 inches from medium coals. Cook 45 to 60 minutes, or until chicken is fork-tender and juices run clear, turning once and brushing frequently with reserved marinade. Discard any remaining marinade.

Yield: 6 servings

Oven Directions: **1.** Marinate chicken as directed. Heat oven to 350°F. Place chicken in ungreased 15 × 10 × 1-inch baking pan.
2. Bake at 350°F. for 45 to 55 minutes, or until chicken is fork-tender and juices run clear, turning once and brushing frequently with reserved marinade. Discard any remaining marinade.

Indonesian Chicken

Nutrition Information Per Serving
Serving Size: ⅙ of Recipe • Calories 420 • Calories from Fat 280 • Total Fat 31 g
Saturated Fat 17 g • Cholesterol 90 mg • Sodium 560 mg • Dietary Fiber 1 g
Dietary Exchanges: 1 Vegetable, 4 Lean Meat, 4 Fat

Herbed Butter-Basted Chicken

Prep Time: 1 hour 10 minutes

Basting Butter
1/4 **cup butter or margarine, melted**
1/2 **teaspoon dried thyme leaves**
1/2 **teaspoon dried sage leaves**
1/4 **teaspoon dried rosemary leaves, crushed**

1/8 **teaspoon garlic powder**

Chicken
3 to 3 1/2 **lb. cut-up or quartered frying chicken, skin removed if, desired**

Grill Directions: 1. Heat grill. In small bowl, combine all basting butter ingredients; mix well.
2. When ready to grill, place chicken, skin side down, on gas grill over low heat or on charcoal grill 4 to 6 inches from medium coals. Cook 45 to 60 minutes, or until chicken is fork-tender and juices run clear, turning once and brushing frequently with basting butter. Discard any remaining butter.

Yield: 4 servings

Oven and Broiler Directions: 1. Heat oven to 350°F. Prepare basting butter as directed above. Place chicken, skin side up, in ungreased 13 × 9-inch (3-quart) baking dish.
2. Bake at 350°F. for 45 to 60 minutes, or until chicken is fork-tender and juices run clear.
3. Transfer chicken, skin side up, to broiler pan. Broil 4 to 6 inches from heat for 2 to 4 minutes, brushing frequently with basting butter. Discard any remaining butter.

Kitchen Tip

Assuming you dip the basting brush into the butter mixture, then onto the chicken as it's cooking, then back into the butter mixture, any remaining uncooked butter mixture should be discarded to avoid contamination from the raw chicken.

Make It Special

Serve the chicken with sprigs of fresh thyme, sage or rosemary.

Menu Suggestion

Round out the meal with steamed green beans, boiled red-skinned potatoes and yellow or red cherry tomatoes. For dessert, offer brownies and ice cream.

Honey Mustard Chicken

Prep Time: 1 hour 10 minutes

Glaze
½ cup apple juice
3 tablespoons Dijon mustard
2 tablespoons oil
2 tablespoons honey
½ teaspoon salt
Dash pepper

Chicken
3 to 3½ lb. cut-up or quartered
    frying chicken, skin
    removed, if desired

About Dijon Mustard

Smooth and complex, this rich-tasting mustard made with wine hails from Dijon, France. Its flavor can range from mild to hot, depending on brands.

Grill Directions: 1. Heat grill. In small bowl, combine all glaze ingredients; blend well.

2. When ready to grill, place chicken, skin side down, on gas grill over low heat or on charcoal grill 4 to 6 inches from medium coals. Cook 45 to 60 minutes, or until chicken is fork-tender and juices run clear, turning often and brushing frequently with glaze during last 15 minutes of cooking. Heat any remaining glaze to a boil; serve with chicken.

Yield: 4 servings

Oven Directions: 1. Heat oven to 350°F. Prepare glaze as directed above. Place chicken, skin side down, in ungreased 13 × 9-inch (3-quart) baking dish. Bake at 350°F. for 30 minutes. Using spoon, remove most of the pan juices; turn chicken.

2. Return to oven; bake an additional 15 to 25 minutes, or until chicken is fork-tender and juices run clear, brushing several times with glaze during last 15 minutes of cooking. Heat any remaining glaze to a boil; serve with chicken.

Nutrition Information Per Serving
Serving Size: ¼ of Recipe • Calories 490 • Calories from Fat 260 • Total Fat 29 g
Saturated Fat 7 g • Cholesterol 135 mg • Sodium 680 mg • Dietary Fiber 0 g
Dietary Exchanges: 1 Fruit, 6 Lean Meat, 2 Fat OR
1 Carbohydrate, 6 Lean Meat, 2 Fat

Island Chicken en Brochette

Prep Time: 45 minutes

8 (12-inch) bamboo skewers
1 tablespoon oil
½ cup finely chopped onion
2 tablespoons brown sugar
¼ cup chili sauce
1 tablespoon lime juice
½ teaspoon salt

½ teaspoon allspice
½ teaspoon ginger
¼ to ½ teaspoon ground red pepper (cayenne)
4 boneless, skinless chicken breast halves

1. Heat grill. Soak bamboo skewers in water for at least 30 minutes.
2. Meanwhile, heat oil in small saucepan over medium-high heat until hot. Add onion; cook and stir until tender. Stir in brown sugar, chili sauce, lime juice, salt, allspice, ginger and ground red pepper. Bring to a boil over medium heat; boil 1 minute. Remove from heat.
3. Cut each chicken breast half into ½-inch-wide lengthwise strips. Add to spice mixture; toss to coat. Weave chicken strips onto skewers.
4. When ready to grill, oil grill rack. Place kabobs on gas grill over medium heat or on charcoal grill 4 to 6 inches from medium coals. Cook 7 to 10 minutes, or until chicken is no longer pink, turning once and brushing frequently with spice mixture.

Yield: 8 kabobs

Nutrition Information Per Serving

Serving Size: 1 Kabob • Calories 80 • Calories from Fat 20 • Total Fat 2 g
Saturated Fat 0 g • Cholesterol 35 mg • Sodium 95 mg • Dietary Fiber 0 g
Dietary Exchanges: 2 Very Lean Meat

Island Chicken en Brochette

Italian Chicken and Potato Packets

Recipe Fact

Grilling foods wrapped in foil is a variation on the classic French technique of cooking **en papillote**—cooking food in packets of parchment paper.

Kitchen Tip

For best results when wrapping food for grilling, use heavy-duty aluminum foil.

Ingredient Substitution

Vary the flavors by using mozzarella in place of Parmesan or sweet potatoes instead of baking potatoes.

Prep Time: 1 hour 10 minutes

2 tablespoons olive oil
½ teaspoon dried Italian seasoning
¼ teaspoon garlic salt
¼ teaspoon paprika

4 bone-in chicken breast halves
½ cup grated Parmesan cheese
2 medium baking potatoes, unpeeled, each cut into 8 lengthwise strips

Grill Directions: 1. Heat grill. In small bowl, combine oil, Italian seasoning, garlic salt and paprika; blend well.
2. Cut four 18 × 12-inch pieces of heavy-duty foil. Place chicken breast half in center of each piece of foil; sprinkle each with 1 tablespoon of the Parmesan cheese. Top each with potato strips. Drizzle oil mixture over potatoes and chicken; sprinkle with remaining ¼ cup cheese. Wrap securely using double-fold seals.
3. When ready to grill, place packets, seam side down, on gas grill over medium-high heat or on charcoal grill 4 to 6 inches from medium-high coals. Cook 40 to 50 minutes, or until chicken is fork-tender and juices run clear, turning packets once during cooking. Open packets carefully to allow hot steam to escape.

Yield: 4 servings

Oven Directions: 1. Heat oven to 400°F. Prepare packets as directed above. Place packets, seam side up, on cookie sheet.
2. Bake at 400°F. for 45 to 55 minutes, or until chicken is fork-tender and juices run clear. Open packets carefully to allow hot steam to escape.

Nutrition Information Per Serving

Serving Size: ¼ of Recipe • Calories 440 • Calories from Fat 170 • Total Fat 19 g
Saturated Fat 6 g • Cholesterol 100 mg • Sodium 430 mg • Dietary Fiber 2 g
Dietary Exchanges: 1½ Starch, 5 Lean Meat, 1 Fat OR
1½ Carbohydrate, 5 Lean Meat, 1 Fat

Jamaican Chile Chicken with Banana Chutney

Prep Time: 20 minutes

Grill Paste
2 tablespoons grated orange
    peel
2 to 3 jalapeño chile peppers,
    seeded, if desired, coarsely
    chopped
1 tablespoon grated gingerroot
1 to 2 tablespoons water
2 teaspoons oil
2 garlic cloves, halved
½ teaspoon allspice

Chicken
4 boneless, skinless chicken
    breast halves

Chutney
1 (9-oz.) bottle (¾ cup) mango
    chutney
1 large ripe banana, coarsely
    chopped
1 tablespoon lime juice

1. Heat grill. In blender container, combine all grill paste ingredients; blend 2 minutes or until smooth. Spread about 1 tablespoon paste evenly over 1 side of each chicken breast half.

2. When ready to grill, oil grill rack. Place chicken, paste side up, on gas grill over medium heat or on charcoal grill 4 to 6 inches from medium coals. Cook 8 to 10 minutes, or until chicken is fork-tender and juices run clear, turning once.

3. Meanwhile, in small bowl, combine all chutney ingredients; mix well. Serve with chicken.

Yield: 4 servings

Tip: To broil, place chicken on broiler pan and broil 4 to 6 inches from heat using times provided above as a guide.

Nutrition Information Per Serving
Serving Size: ¼ of Recipe • Calories 340 • Calories from Fat 50 • Total Fat 6 g
Saturated Fat 1 g • Cholesterol 75 mg • Sodium 180 mg • Dietary Fiber 1 g
Dietary Exchanges: 3 Fruit, 4 Very Lean Meat, ½ Fat OR
3 Carbohydrate, 4 Very Lean Meat, ½ Fat

Recipe Fact
This dish is a variation on Jamaica's signature jerk pork, in which the meat soaks up a spicy marinade and is then grilled.

About Jalapeño Peppers
Jalapeños are hot green (or red, if they're allowed to ripen on the vine) chile peppers. The same oils that give the pepper its heat can irritate skin, so wear rubber gloves or wash hands thoroughly after preparing.

About Chutney
Chutney, a specialty of India, is a mixture of sweet, spicy and tart ingredients used as a condiment or relish. In this recipe, fresh banana and lime juice add sweetness and zing to purchased chutney.

Italian Chicken and Vegetable Grill

Prep Time: 30 minutes
(Ready in 1 hour 30 minutes)

About Italian Dressing

Bottled Italian dressing makes a convenient marinade or basting sauce for chicken. If you wish, you can substitute a garlicky homemade vinaigrette.

Ingredient Substitution

Other vegetables that could be used in place of the zucchini or red pepper include yellow summer squash, yellow or green pepper, onion wedges, mushrooms and halved or quartered new potatoes.

Recipe Variation

Make this dish as directed, then chill it to serve as a cold salad.

4 boneless, skinless chicken breast halves
1 zucchini, halved lengthwise
1 medium red bell pepper, quartered
1 (8-oz.) bottle (1 cup) Italian salad dressing
6 oz. uncooked linguine
¼ cup grated Parmesan cheese

Grill Directions: 1. Place chicken, zucchini and bell pepper in 12 × 8-inch (2-quart) baking dish or large resealable plastic bag. Add ½ cup of the salad dressing; turn to coat. Cover dish or seal bag; refrigerate at least 1 hour, turning chicken once.

2. Heat grill. When ready to grill, oil grill rack. Drain chicken and vegetables, reserving marinade. Place chicken on gas grill over medium heat or on charcoal grill 4 to 6 inches from medium coals. Cook 15 to 20 minutes, or until chicken is fork-tender and juices run clear, turning once and brushing frequently with reserved marinade. While chicken is cooking, place vegetables, cut side down, next to chicken on grill. Cook 14 to 18 minutes, or until crisp-tender, turning once and brushing frequently with reserved marinade. Discard any remaining marinade.

3. Meanwhile, cook linguine to desired doneness as directed on package. Drain; toss with remaining ½ cup salad dressing. Remove chicken and vegetables from grill. Slice vegetables; toss with linguine mixture. Slice chicken breasts into crosswise slices; do not separate slices. Fan chicken slices; arrange over pasta and vegetables. Sprinkle with Parmesan cheese.

Yield: 4 servings

Broiler Directions: **1.** Marinate chicken and vegetables as directed above. Lightly grease broiler pan. Place chicken and vegetables on greased broiler pan.
2. Broil 4 to 6 inches from heat for 15 to 20 minutes, or until chicken is fork-tender, juices run clear and vegetables are crisp-tender, turning once and brushing frequently with reserved marinade. Discard any remaining marinade. Continue as directed above.

Nutrition Information Per Serving
Serving Size: ¼ of Recipe • Calories 500 • Calories from Fat 210 • Total Fat 23 g
Saturated Fat 5 g • Cholesterol 80 mg • Sodium 460 mg • Dietary Fiber 2 g
Dietary Exchanges: 2 Starch, 1 Vegetable, 4 Lean Meat, 2 Fat OR
2 Carbohydrate, 1 Vegetable, 4 Lean Meat, 2 Fat

Italian Chicken and Vegetable Grill

Monterey Grilled Chicken with Kiwi-Papaya Salsa

Kitchen Tip

To ripen a green papaya, place it in a paper bag and allow it to sit at room temperature. It's ripe when it has turned golden yellow and yields slightly to pressure.

Healthy Hint

To cut 4 grams fat per serving, eliminate the cheese.

Menu Suggestion

Complete the meal with warmed pita bread and a pasta salad. Offer meringue cookies with tea or coffee for dessert.

Prep Time: 30 minutes

Salsa
- 1 medium papaya, peeled, seeded, coarsely chopped
- 2 kiwi fruit, peeled, coarsely chopped
- 1 teaspoon chopped fresh cilantro
- ¼ teaspoon crushed red pepper flakes
- 1 teaspoon fresh lime juice

Chicken
- 4 boneless, skinless chicken breast halves
- 1 tablespoon oil
- ¼ teaspoon paprika
- ¼ teaspoon pepper
- 2 oz. (4 slices) Monterey Jack cheese

1. Heat grill. In small bowl, combine all salsa ingredients; toss gently to combine.

2. Place 1 chicken breast half between 2 pieces of plastic wrap or waxed paper. Working from center, gently pound chicken with flat side of meat mallet or rolling pin until about ¼ inch thick; remove wrap. Repeat with remaining chicken breast halves. Brush both sides of chicken with oil. Sprinkle one side with paprika and pepper.

3. When ready to grill, place chicken, seasoned side down, on gas grill over medium heat or on charcoal grill 4 to 6 inches from medium coals. Cook 6 to 10 minutes, or until chicken is fork-tender and juices run clear, turning once. Top chicken with cheese; cook an additional 30 to 60 seconds, or until cheese is melted. Serve with salsa.

Yield: 4 servings

Tip: To broil, place chicken on broiler pan and broil 4 to 6 inches from heat using times provided above as a guide.

Nutrition Information Per Serving
Serving Size: ¼ of Recipe • Calories 280 • Calories from Fat 100 • Total Fat 11 g
Saturated Fat 4 g • Cholesterol 85 mg • Sodium 140 mg • Dietary Fiber 3 g
Dietary Exchanges: 1 Fruit, 4 Lean Meat OR 1 Carbohydrate, 4 Lean Meat

Charcoal Grilled Whole Chicken

Prep Time: 2 hours

1 (3- to 3½-lb.) whole frying chicken
¼ teaspoon salt
½ lemon, cut into wedges
¼ cup fresh parsley sprigs
1 tablespoon oil
½ teaspoon paprika

1. Chicken will be cooked by indirect heat. Center drip pan in bottom of grill; add ½ inch water to pan. Place 25 briquets on left side of pan and 25 on right side. Light charcoal; allow 20 to 30 minutes for coals to reach medium-high heat (to develop a light coating of gray ash).

2. Meanwhile, remove neck and giblets from chicken; discard. Rinse chicken with cold water; pat dry. Sprinkle cavity of chicken with salt. Place lemon and parsley inside cavity. Fasten neck skin to back with skewer. Turn wings back and tuck tips under shoulder joints. Rub outside surface with oil; sprinkle with paprika.

3. When ready to grill, place chicken, breast side up, on grill rack 4 to 6 inches directly above drip pan. Cover; cook 1 to 1½ hours, or until chicken is fork-tender, juices run clear and drumstick moves easily up and down and twists in socket. Let stand 5 to 10 minutes before carving.

Yield: 4 servings

Nutrition Information Per Serving

Serving Size: ¼ of Recipe • Calories 400 • Calories from Fat 230 • Total Fat 25 g
Saturated Fat 6 g • Cholesterol 135 mg • Sodium 260 mg • Dietary Fiber 0 g
Dietary Exchanges: 6½ Lean Meat, 1 Fat

Make-Ahead Tip

The chicken is delicious hot from the grill, but also can be refrigerated for up to two days after grilling. Slice and reheat the meat or enjoy it cold for sandwiches or chicken salad.

Menu Suggestion

Make this meal a summer feast with corn on the cob, pasta salad with vegetables, and a huge bowl of garden greens tossed with vinaigrette, tomato wedges, fresh herbs and red onion slices. For dessert, set out a large platter of fresh berries and slices of melon. Cap off the day with ice cream cones or toasted marshmallows.

Peppered Chicken

Prep Time: 25 minutes

8 boneless, skinless chicken thighs
1 teaspoon dried thyme leaves
¼ teaspoon garlic powder
¼ teaspoon onion salt
¼ teaspoon white pepper
¼ teaspoon ground red pepper (cayenne)
¼ teaspoon black pepper
1 tablespoon oil

Grill Directions: 1. Heat grill. Place 2 chicken thighs between 2 pieces of plastic wrap or waxed paper. Working from center, gently pound chicken with flat side of meat mallet or rolling pin until about ¼ inch thick; remove wrap. Repeat with remaining chicken thighs.
2. In small bowl, combine all remaining ingredients except oil. Brush both sides of chicken thighs with oil; coat with pepper mixture.
3. When ready to grill, place chicken on gas grill over medium heat or on charcoal grill 4 to 6 inches from medium coals. Cook 8 to 10 minutes, or until chicken is fork-tender and juices run clear, turning once.

Yield: 4 servings

Broiler Directions: 1. Prepare recipe as directed above. Place chicken thighs on broiler pan.
2. Broil 4 to 6 inches from heat for 8 to 10 minutes, or until chicken is no longer pink and juices run clear, turning once.

Nutrition Information Per Serving
Serving Size: ¼ of Recipe • Calories 240 • Calories from Fat 140 • Total Fat 15 g
Saturated Fat 4 g • Cholesterol 100 mg • Sodium 200 mg • Dietary Fiber 0 g
Dietary Exchanges: 4 Lean Meat, ½ Fat

Plum Barbecued Chicken Kabobs

Prep Time: 30 minutes
(Ready in 1 hour 30 minutes)

Marinade
½ cup plum preserves
2 tablespoons lemon juice
2 tablespoons soy sauce
1 tablespoon oil
¼ to ½ teaspoon dried sage
    leaves, crushed

Kabobs
4 boneless, skinless chicken
    breast halves, cut into
    1-inch pieces
1 cup seedless red grapes

1. In 12×8-inch (2-quart) baking dish or large resealable plastic bag, combine all marinade ingredients; blend well. Add chicken; turn to coat. Cover dish or seal bag; refrigerate at least 1 hour, turning chicken once.

2. Heat grill. Drain chicken, reserving marinade. Alternately thread chicken and grapes onto five 12-inch metal skewers.

3. When ready to grill, oil grill rack. Place kabobs on gas grill over medium heat or on charcoal grill 4 to 6 inches from medium coals. Cook 10 to 15 minutes, or until chicken is no longer pink, turning often and brushing frequently with reserved marinade. Discard any remaining marinade.

Yield: 5 kabobs

Tip: To broil, place kabobs on broiler pan and broil 4 to 6 inches from heat using times provided above as a guide.

Nutrition Information Per Serving
Serving Size: 1 Kabob • Calories 150 • Calories from Fat 25 • Total Fat 3 g
Saturated Fat 1 g • Cholesterol 55 mg • Sodium 150 mg • Dietary Fiber 0 g
Dietary Exchanges: 1 Fruit, 3 Very Lean Meat OR
1 Carbohydrate, 3 Very Lean Meat

Ingredient Substitution

Peach or apricot preserves or orange marmalade can substitute for the plum preserves.

Make It Special

Garnish the plate with slices of fresh plum and a tiny bunch of grapes.

Menu Suggestion

Serve the chicken kabobs on a bed of hot cooked couscous or a mixture of white and wild rice. Round out the meal with a cool tossed salad and a sautéed or steamed vegetable combination of julienned zucchini, yellow squash, carrots and chopped onion.

Sweet and Spicy Chicken Dinner Packets

Prep Time: 1 hour 10 minutes

½ cup chili sauce
3 tablespoons brown sugar
2 tablespoons fresh lime juice
½ teaspoon ginger
¼ teaspoon ground red pepper
  (cayenne)
2 medium sweet potatoes,
  peeled, cut into thin strips

1 medium green bell pepper,
  cut into thin strips
4 chicken drumsticks, skin
  removed, if desired
4 chicken thighs, skin
  removed, if desired

Recipe Variation

Brush the chili sauce mixture onto a whole roasted chicken or baked chicken parts about 15 minutes before the end of cooking time.

Menu Suggestion

Accompany the meal with steamed fresh sugar snap peas and wedges of hearty sourdough bread.

1. Heat grill. In small bowl, combine chili sauce, brown sugar, lime juice, ginger and ground red pepper; blend well.

2. Cut four 18 × 12-inch pieces of heavy-duty foil. Place ¼ of the sweet potatoes and bell pepper in center of each piece of foil; top each with drumstick and thigh. Spoon chili sauce mixture evenly over vegetables and chicken. Wrap securely using double-fold seals.

3. When ready to grill, place packets, seam side down, on gas grill over medium-high heat or on charcoal grill 4 to 6 inches from medium-high coals. Cook 40 to 50 minutes, or until chicken is fork-tender and juices run clear, turning packets once during cooking. Open packets carefully to allow hot steam to escape.

Yield: 4 servings

Nutrition Information Per Serving
Serving Size: ¼ of Recipe • Calories 420 • Calories from Fat 140 • Total Fat 16 g
Saturated Fat 4 g • Cholesterol 105 mg • Sodium 570 mg • Dietary Fiber 3 g
Dietary Exchanges: 2 Starch, ½ Fruit, 3½ Lean Meat, 1 Fat OR
2½ Carbohydrate, 3½ Lean Meat, 1 Fat

Sweet and Spicy Chicken Dinner Packets

Glazes and Rubs

Glazes and Rubs for Flavor-Packed Grilling and Broiling

Open your cupboard to discover more than a dozen ways to transform a good chicken dinner into a superlative one. The secret: Homemade glazes and rubs, quickly assembled from on-hand ingredients, add incomparable flavor to grilled or broiled poultry.

Glazes are liquidy concoctions that typically contain something sweet (such as honey or preserves) that caramelizes as it cooks, yielding a mouthwatering browned exterior. A sharp ingredient (such as curry, citrus, ginger, hot mustard or salsa) injects a bit of zing and prevents the sweet flavor from becoming overly cloying. To prevent burning, brush the mixture onto the meat about 15 minutes before the end of grilling or broiling time. The glazes are very fast to assemble; none has more than four ingredients. They're best prepared immediately before use so they don't become watery and lose their clinging ability.

Rubs are blends of dry seasonings. Some remain staunchly savory—such as Mexican Dry Rub, p. 247—while others, such as Lemon-Pepper Rub, p. 247, gain a sweet note from brown sugar, cinnamon or another spice. With your fingers, rub the mixture all over the chicken before cooking; work some of it underneath the skin, if the chicken is being cooked with the skin on. This way even if you remove the skin after cooking the rub will still flavor the meat. Since the rubs contain no perishable ingredients, you can mix up a large batch to keep on hand or share with friends. Store the rub in an airtight container in a cool, dry place.

Use these versatile glazes and rubs interchangeably to boost the flavor of any piece of chicken, with or without skin, boneless or bone-in.

Glazes and Rubs

Previous page: Curry Marmalade Chicken page 246

Apple Curry Glaze

¼ cup apple jelly
2 teaspoons curry powder
¼ teaspoon ginger
Dash salt

In small bowl, combine all ingredients; blend well. Grill or broil chicken as desired, basting with glaze during last 15 minutes of cooking time.

Yield: 4 servings

Nutrition Information Per Serving

Serving Size: ¼ of Recipe • Calories 60
Calories from Fat 0 • Total Fat 0 g
Saturated Fat 0 g • Cholesterol 0 mg
Sodium 40 mg • Dietary Fiber 1 g
Dietary Exchanges: 1 Fruit OR 1 Carbohydrate

Apple-Sweet Barbecue Glaze

3 tablespoons frozen apple juice concentrate, thawed
½ cup barbecue sauce

In small bowl, combine ingredients; blend well. Grill or broil chicken as desired, basting with glaze during last 15 minutes of cooking time.

Yield: 4 servings

Nutrition Information Per Serving

Serving Size: ¼ of Recipe • Calories 50
Calories from Fat 10 • Total Fat 1 g
Saturated Fat 0 g • Cholesterol 0 mg
Sodium 260 mg • Dietary Fiber 0 g
Dietary Exchanges: ½ Starch OR
½ Carbohydrate

Caribbean Rub

1 teaspoon garlic powder
1 teaspoon dried thyme leaves
1 teaspoon allspice
1 teaspoon nutmeg
½ teaspoon salt
½ teaspoon mace
½ teaspoon cloves
¼ teaspoon coarsely ground black pepper

In small bowl, combine all ingredients; mix well. Rub mixture evenly on both sides of chicken pieces. Grill or broil as desired.

Yield: 4 servings

Nutrition Information Per Serving

Serving Size: ¼ of Recipe • Calories 10
Calories from Fat 0 • Total Fat 0 g
Saturated Fat 0 g • Cholesterol 0 mg
Sodium 270 mg • Dietary Fiber 0 g
Dietary Exchanges: Free

Curry Marmalade Glaze

½ cup orange marmalade
2 tablespoons lemon juice
½ teaspoon curry powder

In small bowl, combine all ingredients; blend well. Grill or broil chicken as desired, basting with glaze during last 15 minutes of cooking time.

Yield: 4 servings

Nutrition Information Per Serving
Serving Size: ¼ of Recipe • Calories 110
Calories from Fat 0 • Total Fat 0 g
Saturated Fat 0 g • Cholesterol 0 mg
Sodium 25 mg • Dietary Fiber 0 g
Dietary Exchanges: 2 Fruit OR 2 Carbohydrate

French Dressing and Wine Glaze

½ cup purchased reduced-calorie
creamy French salad dressing
¼ cup dry white wine

In small bowl, combine ingredients; blend well. Grill or broil chicken as desired, basting with glaze during last 15 minutes of cooking time.

Yield: 4 servings

Nutrition Information Per Serving
Serving Size: ¼ of Recipe • Calories 60
Calories from Fat 20 • Total Fat 2 g
Saturated Fat 0 g • Cholesterol 0 mg
Sodium 260 mg • Dietary Fiber 0 g
Dietary Exchanges: 1 Fruit OR 1 Carbohydrate

Hoisin and Honey Glaze

⅓ cup hoisin sauce
3 tablespoons honey

In small bowl, combine ingredients; blend well. Grill or broil chicken as desired, basting with glaze during last 15 minutes of cooking time.

Yield: 4 servings

Nutrition Information Per Serving
Serving Size: ¼ of Recipe • Calories 110
Calories from Fat 10 • Total Fat 1 g
Saturated Fat 0 g • Cholesterol 0 mg
Sodium 410 mg • Dietary Fiber 0 g
Dietary Exchanges: 2 Fruit OR 2 Carbohydrate

Lemon-Pepper Rub

2 tablespoons brown sugar
2 teaspoons lemon pepper seasoning
2 teaspoons garlic powder
½ teaspoon ground red pepper (cayenne)

In small bowl, combine all ingredients; mix well. Rub mixture evenly on both sides of chicken pieces. Grill or broil as desired.

Yield: 4 servings

Nutrition Information Per Serving
Serving Size: ¼ of Recipe • Calories 30
Calories from Fat 0 • Total Fat 0 g
Saturated Fat 0 g • Cholesterol 0 mg
Sodium 310 mg • Dietary Fiber 0 g
Dietary Exchanges: ½ Fruit OR ½ Carbohydrate

Lime Salsa Glaze

½ cup purchased thick and chunky salsa
1 tablespoon fresh lime juice
2 teaspoons chili powder

In small bowl, combine all ingredients; blend well. Grill or broil chicken as desired, basting with glaze during last 15 minutes of cooking time.

Yield: 4 servings

Nutrition Information Per Serving
Serving Size: ¼ of Recipe • Calories 20
Calories from Fat 10 • Total Fat 1 g
Saturated Fat 0 g • Cholesterol 0 mg
Sodium 320 mg • Dietary Fiber 0 g
Dietary Exchanges: 1 Vegetable

Mexican Dry Rub

1 teaspoon onion powder
¾ teaspoon seasoned salt
1½ teaspoons dried oregano leaves, crushed
¾ teaspoon crushed red pepper flakes
½ teaspoon garlic-pepper seasoning
½ teaspoon chili powder
¼ teaspoon cumin

In small bowl, combine all ingredients; mix well. Rub mixture evenly on both sides of chicken pieces. Grill or broil as desired.

Yield: 4 servings

Nutrition Information Per Serving
Serving Size: ¼ of Recipe • Calories 0
Calories from Fat 0 • Total Fat 0 g
Saturated Fat 0 g • Cholesterol 0 mg
Sodium 330 mg • Dietary Fiber 0 g
Dietary Exchanges: Free

Mustard and Chili Sauce Glaze

¾ cup chili sauce
¼ cup beer
1 teaspoon dry mustard

In small bowl, combine all ingredients; blend well. Grill or broil chicken as desired, basting with glaze during last 15 minutes of cooking time.

Yield: 4 servings

Nutrition Information Per Serving
Serving Size: ¼ of Recipe • Calories 60
Calories from Fat 0 • Total Fat 0 g
Saturated Fat 0 g • Cholesterol 0 mg
Sodium 680 mg • Dietary Fiber 0 g
Dietary Exchanges: ½ Starch, ½ Fruit
OR 1 Carbohydrate

Peachy Barbecue Sauce Glaze

⅓ cup barbecue sauce
¼ cup peach spreadable fruit
½ teaspoon dried thyme leaves

In small bowl, combine all ingredients; blend well. Grill or broil chicken as desired, basting with glaze during last 15 minutes of cooking time.

Yield: 4 servings

Nutrition Information Per Serving
Serving Size: ¼ of Recipe • Calories 70
Calories from Fat 0 • Total Fat 0 g
Saturated Fat 0 g • Cholesterol 0 mg
Sodium 180 mg • Dietary Fiber 0 g
Dietary Exchanges: 1 Fruit OR 1 Carbohydrate

Spicy Rub

1 tablespoon oil
½ teaspoon onion powder
⅛ teaspoon salt
¼ teaspoon allspice
¼ teaspoon ground thyme
⅛ teaspoon ground red pepper (cayenne)
Dash cinnamon

In small bowl, combine all ingredients; mix well. Rub mixture evenly on both sides of chicken pieces. Grill or broil as desired.

Yield: 4 servings

Nutrition Information Per Serving
Serving Size: ¼ of Recipe • Calories 25
Calories from Fat 25 • Total Fat 3 g
Saturated Fat 0 g • Cholesterol 0 mg
Sodium 65 mg • Dietary Fiber 0 g
Dietary Exchanges: ½ Fat

Spicy Sweet Glaze

**1 (8-oz.) bottle spicy-sweet French
salad dressing**
½ cup apricot preserves
1 to 2 tablespoons dry onion soup mix

In small bowl, combine all ingredients; blend well. Grill or broil chicken as desired, basting with glaze during last 15 minutes of cooking time.

Yield: 4 servings

Nutrition Information Per Serving

Serving Size: ¼ of Recipe • Calories 350
Calories from Fat 180 • Total Fat 20 g
Saturated Fat 4 g • Cholesterol 0 mg
Sodium 1070 mg • Dietary Fiber 1 g
Dietary Exchanges: 3 Fruit, 4 Fat
OR 3 Carbohydrate, 4 Fat

Sweet and Zesty Apricot Glaze

⅔ cup apricot preserves
¼ cup sweet hot mustard

In small bowl, combine ingredients; blend well. Grill or broil chicken as desired, basting with glaze during last 15 minutes of cooking time.

Yield: 4 servings

Nutrition Information Per Serving

Serving Size: ¼ of Recipe • Calories 170
Calories from Fat 20 • Total Fat 2 g
Saturated Fat 1 g • Cholesterol 0 mg
Sodium 160 mg • Dietary Fiber 1 g
Dietary Exchanges: 2½ Fruit, ½ Fat
OR 2½ Carbohydrate, ½ Fat

Thyme and Rosemary Herb Rub

**2 tablespoons chopped fresh thyme or
2 teaspoons dried thyme leaves**
**2 tablespoons chopped fresh rosemary
or 2 teaspoons dried rosemary
leaves, crushed**
1 tablespoon olive oil or vegetable oil
2 teaspoons paprika
1 teaspoon salt
**1 teaspoon coarsely ground black
pepper**

In small bowl, combine all ingredients; mix well. Rub mixture evenly on both sides of chicken pieces. Grill or broil as desired.

Yield: 4 servings

Nutrition Information Per Serving

Serving Size: ¼ of Recipe • Calories 40
Calories from Fat 35 • Total Fat 4 g
Saturated Fat 0 g • Cholesterol 0 mg
Sodium 530 mg • Dietary Fiber 0 g
Dietary Exchanges: 1 Fat

Index